# *abide*

## 40 Ways to Focus on Jesus Daily

# TARA L. COLE

*JUANITA COVERT'S GRANDDAUGHTER*

**Abide: 40 Ways to Focus on Jesus Daily**

Copyright © 2019 Tara Cole

Editors Susan Slaubaugh and Erin Adams

Cover Design by Clarissa Dudley

Formatted by Eswari Kamireddy

Tara Cole is a wife and mother to three active boys. Her passion is helping moms and their kids deepen their relationships with God. Her previous works include *Sacred Pathways for Kids* with Christie Thomas. You can find more of her writing at taralcole.com.

*To my Mom, Cindy Cain, who first taught me by her example what it means to abide.*

# Table of Contents

Introduction ...........................................................................1

1: Listening to the Bible.............................................6

2: Praying While Doing Chores..................................8

3: Having Daily Devotionals................................... 10

4: Listening to Christian Music ............................... 12

5: Practicing Patience ............................................. 14

6: Studying the Bible: LOOK ................................. 18

7: Praying ACTS Prayers ........................................ 22

8: Discovering YouVersion Devotionals .................. 26

9: Joining with a Church ......................................... 28

10: Serving Family .................................................. 30

11: Reading Psalm and Proverbs............................. 32

12: Giving Thanks .................................................. 34

13: Finding Good Books ......................................... 36

14: Journaling the Bible .......................................... 38

15: Learning to Listen ............................................. 40

16: Going Verse by Verse........................................ 42

17: Praying in the Car.............................................. 44

18: Listening to Lessons on Podcast or CD ............. 46

19: Creating Art....................................................... 48

20: Being Kind ........................................................ 50

21: Memorizing Scripture ....................................... 52

22: Doing Family Prayers ....................................... 54

23: Having Family Devotions .................................. 56

24: Doing Service for Others.................................... 60

25: Discovering Bible Promises............................... 62

26: Praying God's Word .......................................... 64

27: Delivering Daily Blessings ................................ 66

28: Hunting Treasure ............................................... 68

29: Discovering the 5 W's and the H................................ 70

30: Sharing Our God Stories...................................... 74

31: Giving to Others ............................................ 78

32: Helping Orphans and Widows................................ 80

33: Reading through the Bible ................................... 82

34: Praying "War Room" Prayers................................ 86

35: Finding Encouraging Websites ............................... 88

36: Studying with Someone...................................... 90

37: Discovering the Context of the Bible.......................... 92

38: Sharing Hospitality......................................... 94

39: Using the Sword of Spirit................................... 98

40: Listening to God ........................................... 100

Congratulations!.............................................. 103

Abiding with Kids............................................. 104

Resources .................................................... 129

Notes ........................................................ 136

# Introduction

I take karate with my boys. Karate takes focus and discipline. Like all sports, it isn't one that you show up for when you feel like it and do well. Twice a week we rush to karate class after school, and often I join the all-adult class at 5:30 in the morning. My two favorite parts of karate are its graceful forms and adrenaline-packed sparring.

When I'm sparring with a partner, it is tempting to look at their hands and feet to block punches and kicks and find an opening. The loud "Kiap" they yell is meant to distract and can make me want to retreat. Counterintuitively, to win the match, my instructors have told me I have to look my partner in the eyes. I have to tune out their loud, fierce "Kiap" and make one of my own.

Our Karate instructors tell me that when I look up look and focus on the eyes everything will become clear. I can better anticipate my partner's next move. They remind me that when I focus on the hands and feet, like I'm tempted to do, I get caught up in the chaos and can't clearly see what is going on in the match. Often they say, "Where the head goes the body follows." When my head is up and focused, my body is too. When my head is looking down, it's not long before I go down.

Abiding is Jesus' invitation to look up. He's inviting us not just to church on Sunday or a quiet time in the morning, though those are very good things. Instead, he's inviting us into a life that is focused on Him, focused up above the chaos, so we can better anticipate and prepare for where he leads us.

Jesus invites us to look up and live in relationship with him. In John 15:4-5, he says,

*"Abide in me, and I in you. As the branch cannot bear fruit by itself, unless it abides in the vine, neither can you, unless you abide in me. I am the vine; you are the branches. Whoever abides in me and I in him, he it is that bears much fruit, for apart from me you can do nothing."*

I love how he compares us to branch on a vine. A branch doesn't just connect once a day or a few times a week and have enough nourishment to survive the rest of the week. It is in constant contact with the Vine. Constantly abiding in Jesus' presence.

What does "abide" really mean? After a quick search you'll learn that it means, "to remain," "to continue to be present," "to be held, kept, continually."[1] Isn't that a beautiful idea? That we are invited to abide in Jesus' presence continually, to be held by him.

It can be so hard to abide with all the constraints on our time. We often feel overwhelmed and like one more to-do would be the end of us. Jesus isn't inviting us to add one more to-do to our already bulging list.

He's asking us to hand the list over to him and let him teach us how to live our days in him and through his strength. He's asking us to put him and his kingdom first, and let him strengthen us for the rest.

This book is your invitation to look up. In it you'll find forty different ways to focus your eyes on Jesus. Some may work for you better than others. Each is a different way to take your eyes off the chaos around you and to place your focus on abiding. To say, "Yes!" to Jesus and look up.

## How to Use This Book

This book began as a list in the margins of my notes from a Bible class I taught at church. I had asked the question, "What does it look like to abide in Jesus?"

The women in class gave me about twenty-five ideas that Wednesday night that I wrote down to help me learn to abide in Jesus myself. As I used them and added them to the list I discovered that, through the practical suggestions of those women, born of years of experience and a wide range of personality types, I was learning how to not *just* have a morning quiet time. I was learning to say "yes" to Jesus' invitation to abide throughout my day.

I couldn't keep this discovery to myself! This book is the product of three years of my own journey learning to look up and abide in Jesus. I can't wait to share it with you!

There are several ways to use this book.

1. **Start from the beginning and do a forty-day challenge** trying one activity each day. The chapters are written to take you less than five minutes to read and the activities take ten minutes or less to do. If you want to spend more time with Jesus, each day's activity is easily expanded.

2. **Spread the activities over eight weeks.** You could do one activity each weekday for eight weeks to give you time to do other studies with your church or small group over the weekend.

3. **Join with a group of friends** and learn how to abide in Jesus together. Often times it helps us to learn in community with others. You could do either of the above ideas or go by topic (See suggestion #6). When we learn in community, it often brings insights we might have otherwise missed, along with accountability and encouragement to keep going.

4. **Study as a family.** In the back of the book, you'll find "Abiding with Kids" ideas for every chapter in the book. If you have children of any age in your life, these ideas can help you learn how to abide in Jesus together. No need to keep up with two separate Bible studies: you all can join together to deepen your relationship with Jesus.

5. **Use the book for ideas as you need them.** I have several favorite study books and devotionals laying with my Bible. (I share those resources later in the book!). When I'm short on time or need a fresh perspective as I look to Jesus, I pick one up and use it for my quiet time that day. These books are just

the espresso shot my abiding time needs. That is the true heart behind this book: to be a resource you turn to again and again to help you learn to abide in Jesus.

6. **Go through the book by topic.** This book has ideas sprinkled throughout for five different ways to abide: in the Word, in Prayer, in Community, in Worship, and in Service. You could take 5 weeks and devote one week to each type of abiding. See the list of each type below.

Whichever way you end up using this book, I pray you commit to saying "Yes!" to Jesus' invitation to abide in his presence. The door is open. Let's walk through it together.

### *Abiding in the Word:*

Ch. 1 "Listening to the Bible"
Ch. 6 "Studying the Bible: LOOK"
Ch. 11 "Reading Psalm and Proverbs"
Ch. 16 "Going Verse by Verse"
Ch. 21 "Memorizing Scripture"
Ch. 25 "Discovering Bible Promises"
Ch. 27 "Delivering Daily Blessings"
Ch. 28 "Hunting Treasure"
Ch. 29 "Discovering the 5 W's and H"
Ch. 33 "Reading Through the Bible"
Ch. 37 "Discovering the Context of the Bible"

### *Abiding in Prayer:*

Ch. 2 "Praying While Doing Chores"
Ch. 7 "Praying ACTS Prayers"
Ch. 17 "Praying in the Car"
Ch. 22 "Praying as a Family"
Ch. 26 "Praying God's Word"
Ch. 34 "Praying 'War Room' Prayers"

## *Abiding in Community:*

Ch. 3 "Having Daily Devotionals"
Ch. 8 "Discovering YouVersion Devotionals"
Ch. 9 "Joining with a Church"
Ch. 13 "Finding Good Books"
Ch. 18 "Listening to Lessons on Podcast or CD"
Ch. 23 "Having Family Devotions"
Ch. 30 "Sharing Our God Stories"
Ch. 35 "Finding Encouraging Websites"
Ch. 36 "Studying With Someone"
Ch. 36 "Sharing Hospitality"

## *Abiding in Worship:*

Ch. 4 "Listening to Christian Music"
Ch. 12 "Thanksgiving"
Ch. 14 "Journaling the Bible"
Ch. 19 "Creating Art"
Ch. 39 "Using the Sword of the Spirit"
Ch. 40 "Listening to God"

## *Abiding in Service:*

Ch. 5 "Practicing Patience"
Ch. 10 "Serving Family"
Ch. 15 "Learning to Listen"
Ch. 20 "Being Kind"
Ch. 24 "Doing Service for Others"
Ch. 31 "Giving to Others"
Ch. 32 "Helping Orphans and Widows"

# Chapter 1
## Listening to the Bible

*"Your word is a lamp to guide my feet
and a light for my path."*

**PSALM 119:105**

Are you too busy to sit down and read your Bible? Do your hands always seem full? Listening to the Bible can help us to abide in Christ no matter how busy we are.

There have been some seasons in my life when I didn't have time to study in the early morning and was so exhausted by bedtime that trying to read the Bible then was hopeless. However, listening to the Bible allows me to connect with God during the spaces of my day.

Whether you're driving to work, eating lunch, nursing a baby, folding laundry, washing dishes…we all have regular stretches in our day where our body is in motion but the task doesn't require much thought. Those are great times to listen to the Bible and abide in Jesus.

You could listen straight through the whole Bible or just listen to one book and stop to think about what you've heard. You could begin to study with a spouse or friend as you listen during the day and discuss at night or over coffee what you both heard.

Even if you do have time for regular Bible study, try listening to the Bible today. Taking every opportunity to draw close and abide in Jesus helps us to hear his voice clearer and connects us to him deeper.

Listening is much easier than you think. Fifteen years ago, my husband had to spend over $100 to purchase the whole Bible on CD. Now it's free! Just download the YouVersion Bible app, find your favorite version, and enjoy listening. Most have a play button towards the bottom of the screen.

Today, I'm praying for you today as you begin listening to the Bible and abiding in Jesus throughout moments of your day. Those moments may seem small and insignificant at first, however, they will add up to so much more over time.

What did you listen to today?

What did you learn?

Did you notice anything that you missed before?

# Chapter 2
# Praying While Doing Chores

*"Pray without ceasing."*

**1 THESSALONIANS 5:17**

Praying while doing chores has been attitude changer for me. I'm not a fan of chores. I know, who is, right? Praying is one way I've found to give me a better attitude in the midst of them, and invite Jesus in, instead of complaining to myself about the fact I have to do them.

Today, while you fold the laundry, clean the kitchen, pick up the house, etc.… try praying for those you're picking up after. As you fold your husband's shirt, say a prayer for him. Thank God for him and pray God guides him throughout the day. This idea is especially helpful if you're upset at the person you're praying for. It's hard to pray for someone and stay angry with them.

If you live alone, this is a good time to pray for your family members who live away from you. Ask God to bless them today and help them through any specific circumstances you know they might be going through.

Also, take the time to pray for yourself, especially, if you're like me and struggle with a good attitude while doing chores. Tell God. Ask him for a better perspective on this type of work. He loves to answer those types of prayers!

## *Abiding*

Try this way of abiding today. What chores are on your list?

Who could you pray for while doing them?

# Chapter 3
## Having Daily Devotionals

*"As a deer pants for flowing streams so pants my soul for you,
O God. My soul longs for God for the living God.
When shall I come and appear before God"*

**PSALM 42:1-2**

Do you struggle to find time to spend with God? Like the Psalmist, does your heart long for time to meet with God?

This is my desire many days. I long for God, but the time is so short. Kids wake up early, a full schedule overwhelms me, someone gets sick, and I sink into bed at night empty, longing for God.

During those times, a good devotional can help sustain you when you're short on time. Devotionals are different from a Bible study because they are short, and you can read them in just a few minutes.

I also find devotionals helpful when I'm struggling to connect with God on my own. When I read his word and it just doesn't sink in, or when I'm so weary I can barely get myself to his feet, having someone else's thoughts and words to guide me helps me to continue to abide and connect deeper with my Father when I don't have time for a longer study.

My favorite right now is the *Hope for the Weary Mom Devotional* by Brooke McGlothlin and Stacey Thacker. I have it laying on my kitchen table, so if a kid wakes up early or I have just a moment to spend with God, I still can get some good quality time in with thoughts to follow me throughout my day.

You can find devotionals in many places. Often your local church will have *Power for Today* or something similar for free, or you can find devotionals by browsing your favorite bookstore whether brick-and-mortar, online, or on the YouVersion app.

Today, find a devotional and try it out. You might even have an unread one laying around your home. Whatever devotional you choose, I pray it gives you new insight into God and gives you a hunger for him as you seek to abide in him daily.

## *Abiding*

There are many great devotionals out there. I have some of my favorites listed as resources below and some come with a Kindle version, too. To abide today go to your favorite Bible app -- YouVersion or BibleStudyTools are two good ones -- and find a devotional series to get you started. On both apps, it's as easy as opening the app and clicking on the "Plans" link at the bottom. I would suggest starting with a short plan, so you feel like you accomplished something, but it's not too overwhelming.

Below you'll find additional suggestions for devotional books.

What plan did you choose?

### Resources

*Hope for the Weary Mom Devotional* by Brooke McGlothlin and Stacey Thacker (Kindle, too)

*God's Little Devotional Book for Women* by David C. Cook

# Chapter 4
## Listening to Christian Music

*"I will give thanks to the Lord with my whole heart;*
*I will recount all of your wonderful deeds.*
*I will be glad and exult in you;*
*I will sing praise to your name, O Most High."*

**PSALM 9:1-2**

When I'm overwhelmed and exhausted, one of the best ways I've found to connect with Jesus is listening to Christian music. We've all been moved by a song sometime in our lives, whether it's a special song that was "our song" with our spouse or one that got us through a hard time in the past.

Christian music has the ability to connect with us in those ways and helps us to abide in Jesus throughout our days. When I was a teenager, listening to songs like Point of Grace's "Jesus Will Still Be There" got me through some very hard days. Listening to Toby Mac's song "Feel It" has helped me connect with my sons as I introduce them to Christian music.

Songs also have the ability to stick with us and play on a continuous track in our heads months or even years after we last heard them. Often God has used songs I've heard years before to encourage me at just the right moment. Even as I write these ideas for you, old church songs like "Nearer my God to Thee" and "Jesus Keep Me Near the Cross" play in my head throughout the day.

No matter what type of music you like, there's a Christian artist out there who sings it. Check out national radio stations like KLOVE or AIR1. You can Google to find others in your area or search phone apps like Amazon Music or Spotify.

Some favorites are Jeremy Camp, Hillsong, Hawk Nelson, and Third Day. These artists are often on a radio station or app.

Today, begin listening to Christian music on a regular basis. The connection it gives you to God and the encouragement it brings will give you hope and lift your spirits even on the hardest days.

## *Abiding*

What songs are your favorites to help you abide in Jesus? Why?

Where will you begin your search for more music to strengthen your walk with Jesus?

**Resources**

*Stations:* KLOVE, AIR1, KXOJ

*Apps:* Amazon Music, Spotify, iTunes

*Artists:*

Point of Grace
Christy Nockels
Jeremy Camp
Hillsong Worship
Hawk Nelson
Toby Mac
Third Day
A Cappella
Vocal Union
Zoe Group

# Chapter 5
# Practicing Patience

*"Love is patient and kind..."*

## I CORINTHIANS 13:4A

The other morning was a typical school morning. Breakfasts chowed down, clothes thrown on, shoes found, backpacks grabbed... all whirling out the door on to another day. Except for son #2. Everyone else was in the car and ready to go while he was still looking for his shoes. Usually, I would rush, rush, rush, him in my actions and words berating him for not moving faster. Then he would dissolve into a puddle on the floor and go to the car in tears because he had failed to move fast enough once again.

This morning, however, the Spirit slowed me down. He whispered in my ear words of patience and kindness. Instead of rushing my son, I waited patiently while he put on his shoes. He jumped up with a smile and bounded out the door ready to face the day, much faster than if I had poured words of condemnation over him.

What a difference patience makes! Practicing patience may not seem like an ideal way to abide in Jesus. It seems hard and sometimes a waste of our time. However, when we abide in Jesus, we not only stay in a close relationship with him, but we also follow his commands (John 15:10) and one of those commands is to love others as he loved us.

I missed that idea until recently. I sought to abide in Jesus through doing fun things like worship and prayer, strolling through his creation and drawing what I saw. I've realized that our abiding in Jesus is shown just as much in the way we love others as it is in the way we love Jesus. Actually, loving others well is loving Jesus well (I John 4:20).

To help us know what love looks like, Paul tells us in 1 Corinthians 13:4-7:

Love is patient and kind. Love is not jealous or boastful or proud or rude. It does not demand its own ways. It is not irritable, and it keeps no record of being wronged. It does not rejoice about injustice but rejoices whenever the truth wins out. Love never gives up, never loses faith, is always hopeful, and endures through every circumstance. (NLT)

Did you catch it? Patience is first. When we seek to abide in Jesus, part of that is being patient with others. Just like with my son, patience can make the difference in a day gone wrong or a day that empowers. Patience can refresh a weary heart, whereas impatience can dry up the heart's strength.

Think back to the last time someone was impatient with you. Do you remember the destructiveness of their words and body language? How their impatience did nothing to help you move forward but only held you back?

Today, let's abide in Jesus by loving others well through the gift of patience.

# *Abiding*

Write down three areas where you're tempted to be impatient.

How can you plan ahead to work toward being more patient at those times? For example, I'm prone to impatience during the morning rush. Doing some tasks at night like getting the boys' lunches ready and placing their backpacks, shoes, and coats by the front door at night helps us stay on time in the mornings. I found getting them up five minutes earlier helps, too.

Write down some ways you can practice patience and set yourself up to be more patient in one of the areas you wrote down above.

Patience can refresh a weary heart, whereas impatience can dry up the heart's strength.

# Chapter 6
## Studying the Bible: LOOK

*"For the word of God is living and active, sharper than any two-edged sword, piercing to the division of soul and of spirit, of joints and of marrow, and discerning the thoughts and intentions of the heart."*

**HEBREWS 4:12**

Just this last week from the Psalms, I learned about how God is my rock and my salvation. I'd heard that idea for years, but that day the reminder about who God is completely changed my perspective about a situation I was struggling with. No, the situation hasn't changed at all, but my heart and perspective on it has in light of who God is. So often I hear from my friends and others, "I want to read God's word, but I just don't know where to start!" It can be intimidating. Many parts can even be confusing and frustrating!

The secret is, you don't have to understand it all right now. The Bible is kind of like layers of earth you dig through, going deeper as you learn. You break the surface the first time you read a passage. Then you hear a sermon, read a book, read other verses, and the next time you read that passage you understand it a little more and other parts of it speak to your heart. That's okay! That's what is supposed to happen.

Unlike other books you read, God's word is living and active (Heb. 4:12). It's not a static book that you read once and understand in full. The truth is if you live to 95, you still won't understand it all. But you'll gain a deeper understanding each time you read it and dig through another layer for the hidden treasure.

The way I've found to help me peel back these layers is to think through my daily study as the word LOOK: Listen, Observe, Open, and Keep.

- **Listen**—This is the passage you're reading today. It can be a whole chapter, several chapters, just a few verses, or a single verse. Just write down what verses you read that particular day. If it's a shorter passage, you might even write out the verses to help you gain more insight. If it's a long passage, you could write out a few of the verses that stood out to you. To gain a deeper understanding, you might even read it in several different versions to help you hear those words anew.

- **Observe**—The simplest way to begin is with the question, what did this passage teach me about God's character and promises? Though many teachers make the whole Bible about us, really it's first about God. He's the author of this letter to us, and we can learn so much about his character through seeking him in his word. The verses may teach you many other lessons; write those down, too, but as you're just starting out, begin with God and you can't go wrong.

- **Open**—We want to open our heart to God and take time to worship him for who he reveals himself to be after we Observe the verses we read. When we worship, it changes us, and we don't want to forget this important step. This could be in song or writing. Whatever way you worship God best.

- **Keep**—To Keep God's word, we want to live it out in our lives. James tells us in James 1:25, "But if you look carefully into the perfect law that sets you free, and if you do what it says and don't forget what you heard, then God will bless you for doing it." Didn't I just tell you the Bible is not all about you and now I want you to live what you just learned? Yes. Sometimes you may see a place where you need to change the way you think or the way you live. That's good! However, if you're beginning with God, learning about him also changes the way you live.

Today, try the LOOK Bible study method. Listen, Observe, Open, and Keep. It can be as simple as that!

# *Abiding*

Use the space below with this study method. You might want to begin with Psalm 23, John 1, or Mark 1.

*Listen:*

*Observe:*

*Open:*

*Keep:*

Sometimes you may see a place where you need to change the way you think or the way you live.

# Chapter 7
# Praying ACTS Prayers

*"And rising very early in the morning, while it was still dark, he departed
and went out to a desolate place, and there he prayed."*

**MARK 1:35**

We know we should pray. We have examples of even Jesus spending
time in prayer. And if Jesus did it, you know it must be important
(Mark 1:35; Luke 6:12). Prayer, at its heart, is being present with God.
We do this while praising him, crying out to him, and coming to him
on the behalf of ourselves and others.

We know Paul taught us to:

"Do not be anxious about anything, but in every situation, by
*prayer* and *petition*, with *thanksgiving*, present your *requests* to God. And
the peace of God, which transcends all understanding, will guard
your hearts and your minds in Christ Jesus." (Philippians 4:6-7, NIV,
emphasis mine).

Did you catch that? We don't just need to present our requests,
though that is one part of it. Instead, we also need to include
thanksgiving. I find that thanking God helps me to remember, even
on the hardest days, who he is, and that he is big and I am little.

One prayer method I've found helpful over the years is ACTS
prayers. I learned it when I first began my own journey to abide in
Jesus daily, and I still find it a helpful way to connect with him.

ACTS stands for:

A—*Acknowledge God*: Here you remember who God is—our
father, creator, redeemer… Often I will take a recent verse from my
Bible study like John 1:14 and pray it back to God to help me
remember who he is.

C—*Confess*: Often in our rush to pray for all the things we need
or want, we forget to confess our sins to God. This is saying, "God,
I've screwed up. I know I've sinned against you in these ways. Please
forgive me."

T—*Thanksgiving*: This is where we remember where our blessings come from and thank God for them. Did you see a recent answer to prayer? Thank him. Did you wake up to a beautiful day? Thank him!

S—*Supplication*: This is a big word that means asking for what we need. It's what we usually do in prayer. Here, ask God for what you need. Pour out your heart to him. Bring the needs of others before him, too.

This way of praying helps me to keep the most important things first. It begins with worship and acknowledging who God is and then ends with my requests of him.

Right now, take a few minutes to pray an ACTS prayer. It may seem simple, but it is powerful.

## Abiding

Let's practice this form of prayer together.

A—Father, thank you for being the God who sees us and wants a personal relationship with us.

C—Please forgive us when we fail to trust you as we should.

T—Thank you for your presence in our lives and for teaching us how to abide in you.

S—Please continue to teach us what it means to abide in you more and more, so we can bear fruit in our lives through your Spirit. In Jesus' name, Amen.

Now use the space below to write down your own ACTS Prayer:

*A—Acknowledge God*

*C—Confess your sins*

*T—Thank God for what he has done*

*S—Supplication*

*Prayer, at its heart, is being present with God.*

# Chapter 8
## Discovering YouVersion Devotionals

*"Come, O children, listen to me; I will teach you the fear of the Lord."*

**Psalm 34:11**

Abiding in Christ can be hard. There are many things vying for our attention, and at times, it can be challenging to find a moment to sit down by ourselves. That's one of the reasons I love the YouVersion Bible app that is available for any smartphone. It brings God's word right to where we are and provides many sound mentors to help us learn more from it.

Go to the YouVersion app on your phone (you can get it free from the App Store or Google Play if you don't have it yet). This app will bring up hundreds of plans for you to choose from. They cover a wide variety of topics and journeys of faith.

Not only does the YouVersion app give you access to hundreds of studies, but it also gives you built-in accountability. On the home page, it suggests friends from your Facebook contacts. Once you're friends with someone, you can see their progress through their Bible studies. Asking a friend to do a YouVersion study with you and working to keep each other accountable through the app would be a great way to help you begin to develop the habit of regular quiet time.

Today, try a YouVersion Bible study. If you're new to Bible study, just scroll down a little and you'll find a whole section of devotionals under the heading "New to Faith." If you've studied the Bible for a while, look for a study by your favorite author, group, or life circumstances.

Using the YouVersion app is a simple way to begin abiding in Jesus right where you are.

## *Abiding*

What study did you choose?

What is one idea you learned from it today?

# Chapter 9
## Joining with a Church

*"I am the vine; you are the branches.*
*Whoever abides in me and I in him, he it is that bears much fruit,*
*for apart from me you can do nothing."*

### JOHN 15:5

When Jesus was talking to the disciples in John 15 about abiding in him, his metaphor was about a branch staying connected to the vine. If you think about it, a vine doesn't have just one branch. Instead, a grapevine has many branches that work together to produce fruit. One branch could never produce enough fruit alone, even connected to the vine. The same is true with us, and one of the best ways to abide in God is in community with others at a local church.

I don't know whether you go to church, just show up, or are actively involved, but joining with others and learning together is how I've grown most in my walk with God through the years.

Churches aren't perfect but neither am I. The important part is to find a church that follows the Bible and seeks after God.

Sometimes finding the right church home can take a few tries. When choosing our last church, we visited several. One, in particular, we'd heard a lot about, but when we walked in no one greeted us, and it was as silent as a tomb. The next Sunday we visited another one, and as soon as we walked in, we were greeted warmly. It felt like coming home, and we've been there ever since.

Today, if you're already plugged into a church family, spend some time praying for them. Pray for your close friends but also those across the aisle and your leaders. Even choose one or two people to reach out to this week and tell them you're thankful for them.

If you're not plugged into a church family yet, spend some time today in prayer about possible choices. Ask God to lead you to a church who will help you draw closer to him and whom you can encourage. Then look up several possibilities and make plans to attend them over the next week or two.

When you find a good church home, they become your village -- a community that helps you learn to abide in God even more. I'm praying for you today as you grow deeper in your community or begin the search to find one.

*Abiding*

Do you have a church home? If so, use the space below to pray for your leaders, friends, and those you don't know well yet.

Who will you reach out to this week and tell how much you appreciate the work they do?

If you don't have a church home, where will you begin your search? Write down two places you'll visit in the next month.

# Chapter 10
# Serving Family

*"As the Father has loved me, so I loved you. Abide in my love. If you keep my commands, you will abide in my love, just as I keep my Father's commands and abide in his love... This is my commandment, that you love one another as I have loved you.*
*Greater love has no one than this, that someone lay down his life for his friends."*

## JOHN 15: 9-10, 12-13

If we want to abide in Jesus, we need to love like he did. These verses immediately follow Jesus' example of washing the disciples' feet as an act of love. In Jesus' kingdom, love equals service.

But service is so hard!

Sure it might be fun to jump in with your local church and serve, but what about your three-year-old at 1:00 in the morning? Your aging parents every afternoon? Your teenager right after a break up? Your husband on a Friday evening after you've both had a long week?

Service to those closest to us often doesn't come at fun or convenient times. That's why a few verses earlier Jesus said, "...apart from me you can do nothing" (John 15:5). He knew the day in and day out service for those closest to us would be hard. Oftentimes we flat out wouldn't want to do it.

Especially in those hard times, we have the chance to draw closer to the heart of God and abide in Jesus by serving in love.

Today, look around for those acts of service you can do for those closest to you. Or when those times come, remember that in those moments you have a chance to grumble or glorify God and abide in Jesus all the more.

## *Abiding*

If there is a time of day or a way that you regularly serve others and tend to see it as a burden, prepare in advance to see Jesus in it. Ask him for his strength, patience, and words to bring encouragement to those you are serving.

# Chapter 11
# Reading Psalm and Proverbs

*"but his delight is in the law of the Lord,*
*and on his law he meditates day and night."*

**Psalm 1:2**

When I first began studying the Bible, one of my favorite ways to study was reading a Psalm and a Proverb each day.

It sounds pretty simple, and it is, but over the years the Psalms have often expressed what I was feeling when little else did. Through many hard times, I have clung to their comfort and promises when I was drowning.

Proverbs, on the other hand, is full of wisdom. When you're not sure what to do or what decision to make, they are a good place to look for sound advice. There have been many times when their wisdom has helped me in relationships.

A few years ago, I used to get offended easily. Then I ran across Proverbs 19:11 which says, "Sensible people control their temper; they earn respect by overlooking wrongs" (NLT). After reading that verse, whenever I was tempted to get upset about something someone said or did, those words would ring in my ears. I'm so glad they did! I came to find out, in many of those circumstances the person's attitude and actions weren't about me at all. They had something else going on, and I had no reason to get upset. It took three years for Jesus to teach me that lesson, but now I can honestly say that it is very hard to offend me.

Today, if you're struggling with a place to start your daily study, or just need to breathe fresh air into your time with God, begin with Psalm 1 and Proverbs 1:1. As you read, pray for insight, note any truths you learn, and consider how you can apply them to your life.

# *Abiding*

Pray for insight into what you will read, then read Psalm 1 or Proverbs 1:1-6. What truths did you learn? What did you learn about God? How can you apply what you learned to your life?

*Listen*

What verses did you choose?

*Observe*

What truths or promises do you find here? What do you learn about how we should relate to others?

*Open*

What do you learn about God and who he is? How can you worship him today?

*Keep*

How can what you learned today change you? Is there an action you should take? Is there an heart change you need to make? Ask for God's help as you study and apply his word today.

# Chapter 12
# Giving Thanks

*"Do not be anxious about anything, but in everything by prayer and supplication with thanksgiving let your requests be made known to God. And the peace of God, which surpasses all understanding, will guard your hearts and your minds in Christ Jesus."*

### PHILIPPIANS 4:6-7

"One, two, three, four count my blessings! One, two, three, four count my blessings!" I love this song by Hawk Nelson called "Thank God for Something." Whenever my family or I am struggling, I like to put it on and play it loud. It's a great reminder of how important it is to count our blessings.

You'll find the same ideas in many Bible passages. Philippians 4:6-7 tells us, "Do not be anxious about anything but in every situation, by prayer and petition, with thanksgiving present your requests to God. And the peace of God, which transcends all understanding, will guard your hearts and minds in Christ Jesus" (NIV). Thanksgiving helps us remember who is in charge. It helps take our focus off ourselves and turn it to the One who is really in control.

Thanksgiving also serves as a reminder of God's faithfulness in the past, which then gives us hope for the future. The Psalms are full of this use of thanksgiving. In Psalm 34 David is praising and thanking God. As he does so, he reminds himself and his readers that God will be faithful again. He writes in Psalm 34:1-4:

"I will praise the Lord at all times. I will constantly speak his praises. I will boast only in the Lord; let all who are helpless take heart. Come, let us tell of the Lord's greatness; let us exalt his name together.

I prayed to the Lord, and he answered me. He freed me from all my fears" (NLT).

When we take time to thank God, even during the hard times, it does the same for us that it did for David. It helps us find his peace, not through our own strength, but by remembering his.

## *Abiding*

One habit that helps me is to write down three things that I'm thankful for each morning. I begin with "Thank you, God, for…" to remind myself of where these blessings actually come from.

Begin today by writing three things you're thankful for in the space below.

*Thank you, God, for...*

# Chapter 13
# Finding Good Books

*"Iron sharpens iron,*
*and one man sharpens another."*

**PROVERBS 27:17**

Sometimes I feel far from God or like I just can't find the right verses for my situation. Reading books others have written feels like they are taking me by the hand and leading me to God.

For years I struggled with the sins between my ears. I know we all do, don't we? Whether it's judging, condescending self-talk, lusting, envying—there are many sins that begin between our ears. I had prayed about my sin, looked for verses, talked to close friends. It felt like I'd done everything to try to overcome it.

Then I attended J.L. Gerhardt's Think Good workshop from which her book *Think Good* stems. The ideas and real applications she gave in the workshop, and then in the book, helped me finally slay that sin. It still rears its head, but now I know I have the weapons to defeat it.

Books are like that. We learn from the author's walk how to abide in Jesus more. We learn from their experience how to find hope and overcome the struggles in our own lives. Oftentimes we learn how to see Jesus.

During some seasons, I use books as my whole quiet time for a while, and during others, I just read them during my weekend quiet time. Either way is good. Just look for books that point you back to God and teach you how to abide in Jesus.

Today, if you have a Christian book lying around you've been meaning to read, go ahead and begin. If you don't have a book on hand, check out some of my suggestions below.

My prayer for you is you will learn more about how to abide in Jesus through the experiences of others.

## *Abiding*

Which book did you choose? What did you learn from it today? Don't forget there are also audio and Kindle books available by many authors.

**Resources:**

*Forgotten God* by Francis Chan

*Think Good* by J.L. Gerhardt

*Goodbye Regret* by Doris Swift

*Fresh Out of Amazing* by Stacey Thacker

*The Mom Walk* by Sally Clarkson

# Chapter 14
## Journaling the Bible

*"I will ponder all your work,*
*and meditate on your mighty deeds."*

**PSALM 77:12**

Bible journaling is one way to Abide in Jesus that I've seen more and more of recently. If you like to paint and journal, there are whole Bible journaling sets available for you through DaySpring and Michaels. However, you don't need to spend money to try this way of abiding today. Grab your Bible, journal, paper, crayons, pencils, pens, whatever you like, and begin to write and draw your favorite verse.

It doesn't have to look perfect and no one has to see it. The point isn't perfection, but connecting with God at a deeper level as you write out or form his words creatively in whatever medium it takes.

As you write the words and add your own pictures and graphics, consider what the words are saying. What do they mean to you? How does illustrating the verse in this way make it come alive for you? What do you learn from it?

As you're creating, you may find yourself thinking more about the words, how they relate to each other, and to you. When I wrote out John 1:4 "The Word gave life to everything that was created, and his life brought light to everyone" (NLT), it made me think about what my life does. Does the life he's given me reflect that light? If so, how?

Today, try Bible journaling. This is one creative way to abide in Jesus our creator. You may be surprised by what you learn and how your relationship with him deepens.

## *Abiding*

Use the space below to begin your own scripture art. Some good verses to start with would be ones in: Psalm 23, Matt. 6:9-13, John 1, or Ephesians 1. If you like, you can post your Bible journaling pictures on Instagram or Facebook with hashtag #abidebook to encourage our whole community.

### Resources

*Inspire Bible*, NLT

Day Springs (they have many great Bible journaling tools)

{in}courage.com has many Bible journaling tools, too.

*The Artisan Pace* by Jeana Saeedi (a coloring devotional)

# Chapter 15
## Learning to Listen

*"Know this, my beloved brothers:*
*let every person be quick to hear,*
*slow to speak, slow to anger;"*

**JAMES 1:19**

Have you ever noticed how much God listens? All throughout the Old Testament, he listened to his people. He listened to their cries for help, to their praise, to their pleas for mercy.

Psalm 34:6 even tells us:

"This poor man cried, and the Lord heard him and saved him out of all his troubles" (ESV).

To follow God's example, part of loving others well and abiding in Jesus is listening.

When we take the time to sit with someone and hear their heart, when we stop and look them in the eyes, we're showing by our actions that they have value to us, that they are important.

I struggle with listening. Often my kids will say something to me, and when I pay attention to my body language, I realize my feet are on their way to another room. My body is facing away from them. My eyes are pointing towards the next thing. In moments like that, I force myself to slow down. I stop, turn around, get down on their level, and look them in the eyes. Then I listen.

Listening isn't always responding with advice or a fix. Sometimes it's showing someone that you hear their heart. Nodding, leaning in, asking relevant questions.

Listening is remembering. When my friend remembers to ask about a struggle I mentioned last week or last month, it means a lot to me. I realize they really listened and heard what I was saying.

Today, focus on listening. Slow down and take time to really hear what your spouse, children, co-workers, and friends are saying. Look them in the eyes while they are talking and shut out the other voices in your head and really listen.

In this way, you'll be Jesus with skin on and abide in him more and more.

## *Abiding*

To learn more about listening, let's look at the examples we see in the Bible. Read over these verses to see how God listened to his people and how Jesus took time to listen to others: Genesis 18:16-33, Psalm 40:1-3, 2 Kings 20:1-11, 2 Chronicles 32:1-23, or John 4.

*Listen*

What verses did you read?

*Observe*

How does God/Jesus listen to his people in this story? How does he show he's heard them?

*Open*

Who is God here? Is there a response you want to make in light of who he is?

*Keep*

What can we learn from his example?

# Chapter 16
# Going Verse by Verse

*"Make me understand the way of your precepts,*
*and I will meditate on your wondrous works."*

**PSALM 119:27**

Priscilla Shirer once said when she had young children, she only made it through a verse a week in her personal quiet time! Hearing that gave me such encouragement. Often we feel abiding in Jesus means devouring and understanding large chunks of his word, when instead it's just as valuable to savor and meditate on a small passage at a time and let it sink into our hearts.

The Psalms and Proverbs are good books for this type of study, as well as many of the books of prophecy in the Old Testament, like Isaiah or Habakkuk, or the letters in the New Testament, like Hebrews or Ephesians. There are many truths tucked into these books that can be lost in a quick read through.

There is no right way to read the Bible verse by verse. You might write a verse out focusing on each section of the passage. Post it around your house or work area for you to think about throughout your day, or journal over what you learn. The important thing is to hear God through his word. What is he teaching you and how can you apply it to your life?

Today, if you feel lost in this Bible study thing, short on time, or are ready to slow down with God and savor his word, try reading just one verse at a time. For those of you in a period of struggle try reading Habakkuk, who asks hard questions of God. Or if you need a reminder of your inheritance in Christ, try Ephesians chapter one.

May God bless you as you savor his word today.

# *Abiding*

Some good places to start for a verse-by-verse reading are the Proverbs or Psalms. Use the space below to do the LOOK Bible study method or another method we've talked about.

*Listen*

What verses did you study? You might try reading the verses in several versions to get a better understanding.

*Observe*

Who is speaking? What other verses does it remind you of in the Bible (your Bible may have cross-references)? What can you learn?

*Open*

What do we learn about God?

*Keep*

How can you apply what you just learned? Change your thinking? Change your actions? Pray for guidance, strength, or help?

# Chapter 17
# Praying in the Car

*"For where two or three are gathered in my name,*
*there am I among them."*

**MATTHEW 18:20**

Praying in the car has helped me connect to God and those I'm praying with much more than I thought it would.

About two years ago, a friend of mine commented during one of our Bible studies on Facebook that she had started praying with her daughter on the way to school. I jumped on the idea since I was running out of time to pray with my sons in the mad dash out the door to school each morning. At first it felt awkward to ask them to pray with me, but now they remind me if I forget.

Praying in the car has had many benefits. First, it gives you a specific time to pray each day. Most of us get into the car at regular times throughout our day, so using that time to pray ensures you won't forget.

Second, if you pray with others while in the car, it gives insight into what is going on in their hearts and lives. When my oldest son recently prayed for kids at school to be kind and speak nicely, I asked him about it afterward and learned some kids at school had been teasing him. He'd never said a word during the regular course of our day, so otherwise, I wouldn't have known at all.

Another benefit when you pray with others is the opportunity to model prayer for them. Praying out loud with my kids has given me the chance to show them how to pray not by telling but modeling.

At other times when I'm alone and praying in the car, it gives me the time to give to God the people and situations in my life. All those "Praying!" comments I make on Facebook, I can pray for in detail. I can hand all the burdens I'm carrying off to God one-by-one.

Today, when you hop in the car whether by yourself or with someone else, take time to pray. This time will allow you to continue to abide in Jesus and even connect to others around you.

## *Abiding*

When will you pray in the car today? Who will be with you (if anyone)? How might you begin the conversation and ask them to pray with you? For our family, we pray on the way to school as soon as we pull out of the driveway. I tell the kids this is a time it's okay to pray with your eyes open.

If you tried this way to abide, whether by yourself or with someone else, will you try it again? What did you learn from the experience?

# Chapter 18
## Listening to Lessons on Podcast or CD

*"Follow the pattern of the sound words that*
*you have heard from me, in the faith and love*
*that are in Christ Jesus."*

**2 TIMOTHY 1:13**

Listening to podcasts or short devotionals on a CD is one of my favorite ways to abide in Jesus.

Many mornings I've just needed a friend to come alongside me and give me a hug (or a kick in the pants!), and often God has used the words of a speaker to encourage me.

My current favorite podcasts are *At Home with Sally* by Sally Clarkson, *Chatologie* by Angie Elkins, *Glorious in the Mundane* by Christy Nockels, and *Out of the Ordinary* by Lisa-Jo Baker and Christy Purifoy. My favorite CD is *Lifeway Women Devotions, Vol. II*. All of these make me feel like I'm connecting with an old friend over coffee. They give me a place of rest, help point me back to God, and keep me on the path.

Sally Clarkson's podcast often does this for me. It is a podcast geared toward Christian mothers and I love that, in a world where I hear "achieve more, do more, be more," she reminds me my most important responsibility is my children. In those relationships, she points me to God for wisdom, and I need that reminder frequently.

Today, go find this type of encouragement. I've listed my favorites above and a few more in the resources below, but there are many more out there for you to try. Begin by searching your podcast app, like iTunes or Overcast, for your favorite Christian authors or by keyword. As you listen, make sure the speakers are grounded in God's word and encourage you to seek a deeper relationship with him.

## *Abiding*

List the podcasts you found. Did you listen to one today? What did you learn from it to help you abide in Jesus more? I'd love to hear about the podcasts you enjoy and what you learn from them. Please share on social media with #abidebook.

### Resources

*Keys for Kids*—Keys for Kids Ministries

*At Home with Sally*—Sally Clarkson

*Chatologie*—Angie Elkins

*Glorious in the Mundane*—Christy Nockles

*Lifeway Devotions Vol. II*—CD

*Abide in Christ*—Andrew Murray (reading of the book)

*God Centered Mom*—Heather MacFadyen

*Out of the Ordinary*—Lisa-Jo Baker and Christy Purifoy

# Chapter 19
# Creating Art

*"When I look at your heavens, the work of your fingers,*
*the moon and the stars, which you have set in place,*
*what is man that you are mindful of him,*
*and the son of man that you care for him?"*

**PSALM 8:3-4**

Creating with art materials or paints is another way to connect with God, the ultimate creator.

Whenever I see a beautiful sky, something inside of me longs to mimic my Father and recreate it. Some ideas I consider for a quilt and others for a painting. Not that I'm a painter, but as a child shadows his or her father, I want to shadow mine. I want to recreate the beauty I see and connect to the One who made it.

Today, look at the world and people around you. How could you use art to recreate what you see and connect with God? As you gather your materials and create, think about God. What can you learn about him by recreating what he has made?

For example, when I see a sunset, I just have to recreate it. It reminds me God creates beautiful sunsets on hundreds of thousands of planets every single day that no one sees. It seems like a lot of beauty gone to waste, but I've noticed as I've observed this world God often saves his most beautiful art for secret places—the center of a flower, the inside of a seashell, a mountaintop. He's not concerned about anyone's applause, and it makes me think, maybe I shouldn't be either. There are many lessons like this one to learn just by observing God's creation.

As you create, don't limit yourself to just painting. Quilting, pencils, photography, clay, play dough, paper mache, woodworking, whatever your favorite way to create is, give yourself permission to do it today and expect to find God waiting there.

## *Abiding*

Go do it! Create in your favorite medium. Then you can jot down here what you learned from the experience. You can share pictures of it at #abidebook on Facebook and Instagram. I'd love to see them!

# Chapter 20
# Being Kind

*"Be kind to one another, tenderhearted, forgiving
one another, as God in Christ forgave you."*

**EPHESIANS 4:32**

When kindness and thoughtfulness are directed at us, we feel loved.

When I walk out of my house and notice that my husband left me the larger car to take the kids to school, even though he prefers it, I feel loved.

When my son walks in the kitchen as I'm feeling overwhelmed by the mess and asks if he can help, though I am tempted to complain, I feel appreciated.

When a friend drops by with my favorite Starbucks, just as I was beginning to drown in laundry and housework, I feel seen.

Kind acts like these help to keep us afloat on the hardest of days and make good days even better.

How often, though, are we caught up in our own days that we forget to be kind? Forget to let that car in front of us in the pickup line? Forget to smile at the frazzled checkout person? Forget to slow down and breathe before we answer our child or spouse from a place of stress that has nothing to do with them?

So often Jesus gives us the ultimate example of kindness when we are weary. In John 4:6 the writer tells us that Jesus was tired from their journey and sat down at the well while his disciples went into the town to buy bread. Just then the Samaritan woman approached the well. Jesus could have ignored her. He could have just let the moment pass, which was the expected reaction, but instead he reaches out to her.

The rest of the story of John 4 tells how eventually many Samaritans believed in Jesus because of the woman's testimony—because of Jesus' kindness.

Today, remember to be kind. Take time to slow down and consider the other people around you. Do they need a smile, soft words, time? Do they need to feel seen by your thoughtfulness? How can you be kind today?

## *Abiding*

Write down two or three people you might come into contact with today, or if you're not leaving the house, two or three people you might reach out to.

Think of ways to be thoughtful and kind towards them today. Does your friend need her favorite coffee? Does your husband need a big hug when he comes home? Do your children need cookies after supper or maybe you to sit with them and hear about their day? Write down your plan below. Kindness towards others takes being intentional. Be intentional today.

# Chapter 21
# Memorizing Scripture

*"I have stored up your word in my heart,*
*that I might not sin against you."*

**PSALM 119:11**

Yes, we've all heard about the importance of memorization. Many of us have memorized verses during our lives, but memorization often gets lost when life gets busy.

When I was little my Mom had us memorize many, many verses, and I hated it. I told her when I grew up, I wasn't going to do it and for years I didn't. It wasn't until several years ago, when those verses I'd memorized as a child came back to me at needed moments, I realized the value of memorizing God's word.

One of the best uses of God's word is fighting Satan's lies. Satan loves to tell us we're not good enough, but we can fight that lie with God's truth like, "For he chose us in him before the creation of the world to be holy and blameless in his sight" (Eph. 1:4, NIV).

If you're struggling with a sin like lust, fight it with verses like, "I made a covenant with my eyes not to look lustfully at a young woman [man]…" (Job 31:1, NIV).

If you're in a dark time remember, "But the Lord has become my fortress, and my God the rock in whom I take refuge" (Psalm 94:22, NIV). Allow his truth to set you free (John 8:32).

If you're new to Bible study, you may be thinking, I don't know enough of the Bible to even know where to turn for verses like these. As you go through the ways to abide we talk about in this book, you'll begin to find verses that jump out at you. Highlight or underline those in your Bible and make a list of verses you want to memorize. The front or back cover of your Bible is a great place for this list!

If you need a verse right now for a specific situation, websites like biblegateway.com allow you to search by topic. You can also use my favorite chapter of the Bible, Psalm 139. It's short and reminds us God is always with us.

Today, find just one verse and begin to hide God's word in your heart. I'm praying for you as you abide in Jesus and begin to memorize his truths.

## *Abiding*

If you need a verse to memorize begin with:

Psalm 139:1(NLT): "O LORD, you have examined my heart and know everything about me."

Or Proverbs 15:1 (CBS): "A gentle answer turns away anger, but a harsh word stirs up wrath."

If you have one in mind, write it out below. Pay attention to the words as you copy it. Also consider posting it around your house in different places. I have a chalkboard that we write our family memory verse on each month. It helps to keep it front and center.

## Resources

*SHARPEN Your Sword* 7-day Memory Verse Ecourse: taralcole.come/shop

GraceNotes, Kid Notes, and Man Notes (monthly memory verse subscription): gracenotessubscription.com

# Chapter 22
# Doing Family Prayers

*"Pray then like this:*
*'Our Father in heaven,*
*hallowed be your name.'"*

**MATTHEW 6:9**

When you pray together as a family, just like studying together, it helps you get to know each other deeper. My sons may not say much about how their day went at school, but sometimes I learn more about what's going on through their prayers. Especially as they get older, hearing their prayers allows me to see their hearts.

Family prayer time is also a good time to model different types of prayers for your children beyond the "God is great, God is good…." Often I pray with my kids to teach them by example how to pray. The Lord's Prayer in Matthew 6:9-13 is a good place to begin or use the acronym PRAY:

P (Praise & Thanksgiving)

R (Repentance for wrongdoing)

A (Ask for you and others)

Y (Yes! All God's promises are "Yes" in Jesus—pray scripture).

Whichever way you choose, don't get caught up in thinking one is the best way. Praying is just like talking and listening to a good friend. As I pray with my sons, I try to balance "it's just talking to someone you love" with "how much of an honor it is to come to the God of the universe and speak with him." We need to be respectful but comfortable.

Try to find a regular time in your day or week to pray together. At times, we have prayed at meals or at bedtime, while during other seasons, praying in the car on the way to school has worked better. We've also combined several times throughout our day to help our sons see that you can come to God anytime and as many times a day as you want.

Also, let your kids hear you pray. It is good for them to listen to how both Dad and Mom pray and talk to God. While it is important to respect your husband as the spiritual leader of your household, often the daily teaching falls to Mom. Pray in front of your kids and let them see you have real conversations with God, which helps strengthen their own faith and prayer life.

As you're praying with your family, it's important to not force your kids to pray. My sons have had seasons when they have chosen not to pray and that's okay. As long as they sit and listen to the rest of us pray, I feel they are still present and learning.

Also, don't pressure yourself into thinking it has to be formal. Just relax and enjoy the time together with God as a family.

## *Abiding*

Today, plan to pray with your family or a friend. Who will you ask? When will you pray? Begin and see how your relationships grow over time in your family, friendship, and with God.

## Resources

*Peter's Perfect Prayer Place* by Stephen Kendrick and Alex Kendrick (for ages 3-7)

*Prayer Journal* by JL Gerhardt (for ages 7-12)

*Prayer in Practice* by JL Gerhardt

*Made to Pray* by Christie Thomas (ebook available on her website: christiethomaswriter.com)

*Pray Like This: A Guided Prayer Journal for Kids* by Liz Millay

# Chapter 23
# Having Family Devotions

*"You shall teach them diligently to your children,*
*and shall talk of them when you sit in your house,*
*and when you walk by the way, and when you*
*lie down, and when you rise."*

**DEUTERONOMY 6:7**

It's great for me to abide in Jesus daily and to walk in relationship with him, but if I never pass that relationship on to my kids, then we will have missed something precious. Family devotions are one of the many ways I model living in a relationship with God for my children.

There is no pressure here. For my toddler, I just read a story from one of his Bible books. Sometimes we read through his whole Bible storybook one night at a time. At other times we choose one story at random.

For older kids, a variety of ideas work:

- Bible stories and devotionals on their level
- Read straight from the Bible starting with Genesis
- Read parts of John looking for who Jesus is in each story
- Bible studies like *The Armor of God* by Priscilla Shirer
- Read through Proverbs a few verses each night
- Do the Abide suggestions in this book (Full list of Abide Kid ideas in back of book)

There is no wrong way to study the Bible with your family.

A tip here. For years I've struggled to keep three boys still while doing our devotional. Some nights they sit on my lap and look at the pictures, but at other times, it's been a real challenge. After reading Sarah Clarkson's book, *Caught Up In A Story,* I got the idea to let my boys draw, color, or play with Legos while listening. As long as they can answer a few questions afterwards, I figure it works. They're no longer running around while I'm trying to read, and they are getting the foundation for what will be their own daily walk later in their lives.

Also, like family prayer time, don't stress over a family devotional time. I've done all times of the day depending on the season we were in. Right now, we have family devotions before bed, but at other times, I've done during breakfast or lunch. Just find a consistent time that works best for your family.

Today, begin abiding in Jesus as a family. If you already have Bible storybooks on your kids' level, begin there, or you can even just begin with Genesis. "In the beginning God created…" and watch him create something beautiful over the years out of this time spent abiding as a family.

## Abiding

Make a plan. When will you begin a regular habit of devotional time with your family?

Where will you do it? Living room, bed room, play room, kitchen table…?

What will you study? I have more suggestions below, or you can begin with your favorite book of the Bible.

Do you need special supplies to help keep young kids busy? Crayons, Legos, building blocks?

## Resources

Here are some of my favorites to get you started:

*Candle Bible for Toddlers*

*Playtime Devotions*

*100 Bible Heroes and 100 Bible Songs* by Stephen Elkins

*Pray and Play Bible*

*Day by Day Kids Bible* by Karyn Henley

*The Jesus Storybook Bible*

*The Armor of God for Young Kids* by Priscilla Shirer

*Wise for Salvation* by Christie Thomas

*Made to Pray* by Christie Thomas (ebook on her website: ChristieThomaswriter.com)

*Indescribable: 100 Devotions about God and Science* by Louie Giglio

It's great for me to abide in Jesus daily
and to walk in relationship with him, but
if I never pass that relationship on to my
kids, then we
will have missed something precious.

# Chapter 24
# Doing Service for Others

*"And this is his commandment, that we believe in the name
of his Son Jesus Christ and love one another, just as he has commanded
us.
Whoever keeps his commands abides in God, and God in him..."*

## 1 JOHN 3:23-24

Abiding in Jesus is good! As we connect deeper with him each day, it can bring us such joy, but if we never get past ourselves and horde that joy, then we're not abiding in Jesus fully.

James 1:27 tells us, "Pure and genuine religion in the sight of God the Father means caring for orphans and widows in their distress and refusing to let the world corrupt you" (NLT). In the Old Testament in Isaiah 58, God condemns Israel for going through the motions and appearing religious, but not actually treating others kindly in their day-to-day lives:

"No, this is the fasting I want: Free those who are wrongly imprisoned; lighten the burden of those who work for you. Let the oppressed go free, and remove the chains that bind people. Share your food with the hungry, and give shelter to the homeless. Give clothes to those who need them, and do not hide from relatives who need your help. Then your salvation will come like the dawn, and your wounds will quickly heal. Your godliness will lead you forward, and the glory of the LORD will protect you from behind" (Isaiah 58:6-8, NLT).

As these verses in the Old and New Testaments show, helping others isn't just a good thing to do but is essential in the life that is seeking to abide in Jesus. God goes where the hurting people are. He did it as Jesus, and he asks us to do it as his followers.

Serving others can take a hundred different forms. It can be taking a meal to someone who needs it. It can be giving time and money to a cause close to your heart. It can be giving away a pair of shoes you just bought to a person who may need them more. It can be raking a neighbor's leaves. It can be driving someone to appointments who can't drive themselves.

My friends and I recently had a yard sale to benefit another friend who has Lyme's disease, and my sister and brother-in-law take a yearly trip to serve in Romania. Serving with others helps connect you to each other and the heart of God.

As you spend time with God today, ask him to open your eyes to all the opportunities around you to serve. Then dive in. You may not feel comfortable at first, and you won't be able to help everyone, but helping even one person can make a big difference. God loves people, and as his followers, we should see and love them, too.

## Abiding

Pray and make a plan. Ask God to open your eyes to the needs around you. Then write your plan and give it a date in the space below.

# Chapter 25
# Discovering Bible Promises

*"I will also praise you with the harp*
*for your faithfulness, O my God;*
*I will sing praises to you with the lyre,*
*O Holy One of Israel."*

**PSALM 71:22**

There are days when you really need encouragement. When it's hard to connect with God yourself or believe that his promises are true. These times are when I love to turn to Bible promises.

Bible promises often give you a new perspective and a shot of encouragement when you need it. You can find Bible promises all the way through scripture. Ephesians 1 is chock full of promises for those who follow Jesus. Ones like:

"In him we have redemption through his blood, the forgiveness of sins, in accordance with the riches of God's grace that he lavished on us. With all wisdom and understanding..." Eph. 1:7-8, NIV

Besides the apostles' letters, there are also many promises to be found in the Psalms, the Prophets, and the Gospels. I have found it helpful to underline the promises I find in a special color as I read my Bible. That way when I need them, I can open my Bible, and they will leap off the page at me.

I also have a couple books of promises like *Joy for the Journey* with various authors, and *God's Inspirational Promise Book* with Max Lucado. These have been especially helpful for finding promises on a certain topic or struggle when I needed them. Both of these books give a few promises from the Bible on the topic and include a very short devotional thought from the author.

Whether straight from the Bible or another book, these promises give encouragement to help you through your day.

# *Abiding*

Today, begin underlining or marking in some way the promises you find in your Bible. If you have a particular struggle, do a search through your Bible on that topic or pick up one of the books mentioned above to be reminded of God's truths.

You may also begin with Ephesians 1. Write down the ones that stand out to you the most in the space below.

## Resources

YouVersion App

Blue Letter Bible App

Bible Study Tool App

Biblestudytools.com

Biblegateway.com

# Chapter 26
# Praying God's Word

*"so shall my word be that goes out from my mouth;*
*it shall not return to me empty,*
*but it shall accomplish that which I purpose,*
*and shall succeed in the thing for which I sent it."*

**ISAIAH 55:11**

Prayer seems so simple but often feels so hard. One of the most powerful ways I've learned to pray is praying scripture. We read in the Bible about how powerful God's word is (Hebrews 4:12), and when we pray that word back to God, we're agreeing with him. We're saying, "God, I believe what you say is true."

I like to use scripture in this way when I'm praying for myself or for others. For example, if I'm trying to avoid responding to my children in anger, I might pray James 1:19:

*God, please help me to be "quick to listen, slow to speak, and slow to become angry" (NLT). I know that anger doesn't bring about your will and words spoken in anger can be very hard for my children to forget. In Jesus' name, Amen.*

It's also helpful to pray God's word when you don't know what to pray. Sometimes circumstances bring us to our knees and praying the Psalms, Job, Lamentations, or verses from another book of the Bible that resonate with you can help give words to the emotions you're feeling.

Today, let's pray God's word back to him. Find verses by searching keywords in your Bible app or a website like biblegateway.com that relate to a struggle you or a loved one is having, or find verses that help give words to what you're going through today. Then pray those words back to God.

If you're new to Bible study and aren't sure where to start, try Jeremiah 29:13. It says, "You will seek me and find me when you seek me with all your heart" (NIV).

No, these words aren't magic, but I have seen God's word work powerfully in my own life when I pray it back to him, and I know it can do the same in yours.

## *Abiding*

Write down the scripture(s) you're praying today. Use the space below to personalize them like I did above with James 1:19.

**Resources**

Some of my favorite resources for praying scripture over my children are:

*Praying for Boys* by Brooke McGlothlin.

*Be Strong in the Lord* and *The Lord is their Shepherd* both by Betsy Duffey and Laurie Myers.

*Pray the Word Journal* by Million Praying Moms at praythewordjournal.com

# Chapter 27
# Delivering Daily Blessings

*"The Lord bless you and keep you;*
*the Lord make his face to shine upon you and be gracious to you;*
*the Lord lift up his countenance upon you and give you peace."*

**NUMBERS 6:24-26**

When you're short on time, another way to abide in Jesus is daily blessings. These are words you speak over yourself or others that pour blessings into their heart and life. They give those you bless courage to keep going, strength for hard days, and help them connect to God.

You can find many blessings already in the Bible. Ones like Numbers 6:24-26 above. You can also turn verses into a blessing like Joshua 1:9:

May you, "Be strong and courageous! Do not be afraid or discouraged. For the Lord your God is with you wherever you go" (NLT).

Daily blessings don't have to be directly from the Bible, though, Susie Larson has a daily blessing that she sends via email each day that is based on Bible thoughts. Her Daily Blessing is free, and you can subscribe at: susielarson.com/email-subscription/.

Just yesterday her words helped me to think, "Okay, I can do this!" during a challenging part of my day. I have even forwarded them on to friends who I knew could also use the encouragement.

Though short, I have seen these blessings encourage my heart and the hearts of my family and friends.

Today, try out this quick way to stay connected to God.

## Abiding

Some of my favorite blessings come right from the Bible. Here's one for you to reflect on today:

"May Christ make his home in your heart as you trust in him. Your roots will grow down into God's love and keep you strong. And may you have the power to understand, as all God's people should, how wide, how long, how high, and how deep his love is. May you experience the love of Christ, though it is too great to understand fully. Then you will be made complete with all the fullness of life and power that comes from God." Eph. 3:17-19, NLT

What thoughts does this blessing bring to mind? What parts of it encourage your heart?

# Chapter 28
# Hunting Treasure

*"Oh that my ways may be steadfast*
*in keeping your statutes!*
*Then I shall not be put to shame,*
*having my eyes fixed on all your commandments."*

**PSALM 119:5-6**

In Chapter 6, we talked about the LOOK method of Bible study. Hopefully, you've had a chance to try it.

Now let's add in a few ideas to help you dig deeper for more treasure.

Some of the books of the Bible tell you what they are about. Reading through John 1, you'll learn that John's themes are to show how Jesus is the light and life, grace and truth, and how he reveals God to us. John 20:31 tells us that John wrote the book so we may believe in Jesus. Once you know the author's themes, you can look for them throughout the rest of the book. It's amazing what I've learned reading John and looking for those themes.

In other books of the Bible, the theme and main ideas aren't so obvious. That's where an introduction to that book of the Bible is helpful. Many Bibles have introductions to the individual books. If yours does, read it to learn the main themes of the book and look for those as you study.

If your Bible doesn't have an introduction to the books, check out biblestudytools.com and click on the book you'd like to study to access an introduction to the book. On the YouVersion app, the NIV version also has introductions to the books. Just click on the "i" on the chapters' selection screen.

As you dig deeper, you might even highlight, underline, or write down each theme as you discover them in the book. When I do this, I begin to see patterns in the message the writer is sharing.

Try digging deeper by exploring a book's themes today. You might be surprised just how much you learn!

## *Abiding*

What book would you like to study today? If you're not sure, try the book of John. You might mark one or all of the following: the words light, life, grace, truth, believe, and ways you see Jesus revealing God. In my study notes in the "Observe" section I wrote, "Light and life?" "Grace and truth?" "Reveal God?" As I read through John, I wrote down instances of Jesus doing any of those things.

Use the space below to get started. What treasure are you seeking in your reading today? What did you find?

*Listen:*

*Observe:*

*Open:*

*Keep:*

# Chapter 29
# Discovering the 5 W's and the H

*"Deal bountifully with your servant,*
*that I may live and keep your word.*
*Open my eyes, that I may behold*
*wondrous things out of your law."*

**PSALM 119:17-18**

When we study the Bible, we're often tempted to think, "How does this apply to me?" But as I'm beginning to learn, the Bible isn't all about me. It's about God. When we look at it from that viewpoint, we need to get to know the context of the stories we're reading. We need to see what God is doing in the lives of the people in them.

It seems counterintuitive that we will change when we take the focus off ourselves. But when we get a clearer picture of who God is and what he's doing, it will change us.

So today, we're going to take a trip back to grade school and remember the 5 W's and the H.

They are: Who, what, where, when, why, and how.

Let's see what the 5 W's and the H look like in practice in one of my favorite stories, Jesus calming the storm in Matt. 8:23-27:

Who—Jesus and the disciples

What—Traveling in a boat after a day of healing the crowds

Where—On the Sea of Galilee

When—Around 30/31 AD near the beginning of Jesus' ministry

Why—The disciples were scared because of the storm

How—Jesus calmed the storm with just his words

When I break the story down like this, I'm reminded that Jesus is all powerful. He can control the storm. He is someone I can trust. When I first seek Him in the words I read, it changes me: not only are my actions prompting me to go DO something, but it first changes my heart.

Today, try the 5 W's and the H on a passage you're familiar with. See how focusing on the context and God helps to change your perspective on those verses and in the process, your heart.

## Abiding

What is one of your favorite Bible stories? You might start with Jonah 1 or Esther 1. Consider that passage in light of the 5 Ws and the H.

Who is in the story?

Where is it taking place?

When is it happening? (Hint: the introduction to the book you're reading might have this information.)

What are they doing? What is God doing here?

Why are they doing it? Why is God acting in this way/saying these words?

How does the story/situation resolve itself?

*...the Bible isn't all about me. It's about God.*

# Chapter 30
## Sharing Our God Stories

*"We will not hide them from their children,*
*but tell to the coming generation*
*the glorious deeds of the Lord, and his might,*
*and the wonders that he has done."*

**PSALM 78:4**

As a new mom, I read all the books. The ones on how to get my baby to sleep, how to be a good parent, how to... you name it. My first son was pretty compliant and went by the book. He followed the expectations of the sleep book exactly and was sleeping through the night by twelve weeks. (This was after eight weeks of not sleeping at all and nursing every forty-five minutes. I kid you not.)

While waiting for my second son to be born, I was exhausted. The only thought that got me through the last few months of pregnancy was that I would implement the sleep solution that worked with his older brother and he would be sleeping through the night by October, two months after he was born.

Well, he took the book and chucked it at me. Actually, he's taken most of my parenting books and chucked them at me. While my first is a by-the-book kid, my second colors all over them and teaches his older brother to do the same.

For years I floundered, wondering how in the world I would get them to grow up to be good, Godly men. Then I heard a God Story.

It was the God Story Kristie Dye shared with my readers and me about her parenting experiences. In it, she talks about being a student of your children. Of intentionally watching them and getting to know them as individuals, so you can parent them intentionally.

Her story changed mine. With my first two boys and now my third, I work to parent them as unique individuals.

I see how much my oldest likes to analyze, and I try to communicate and catch his heart in that language. I notice how my middle son loves nature, so I point out God's creation to him. I watch how my youngest loves to entertain, so I embrace it and give him opportunities to make others smile. From hearing Kristie's God Story, I learned that if I tried to relate to all my sons the same, it would spell disaster for their hearts.

Stories, especially God Stories, have the power to speak to our hearts where nothing else can. In the Bible we see stories of Jesus transform vague theological concepts into flesh and blood reality. They help us see how to practically apply what we're learning.

In Psalm 78:1-2 & 5-8 Asaph emphasizes the importance of sharing our stories. He tells Israel to share these stories with their children so they would put their trust in God and keep his covenant.

When we remember our God Stories from the past, we strengthen our resolve to be faithful to God in the future. When we hear God Stories from others, they help us trust that God will provide in our own lives.

## *Abiding*

I have a God Story journal for our family. Whenever God "shows up" in a very real way, I write down the story. That way when we look back, we can see that God was with us in the past, and trust he'll be with us in the future.

Today, journal, scrapbook, videotape, share a God Story from your life or someone you know. Begin a regular way to keep track of your family God Stories so you can look back years later and remember God's faithfulness.

Don't think every God Story needs to be life changing. He loves to show up in the middle of our days in little ways too, through just the right song, rainbow, image... write down your God Stories both big and little.

**Resources**

Find God Stories on taralcole.com/godstories

When we remember our God Stories from the past, we strengthen our resolve to be faithful to God in the future.

# Chapter 31
## Giving to Others

*"But if anyone has the world's goods and sees his
brother in need, yet closes his heart against him,
how does God's love abide in him?"*

**1 JOHN 3:17**

If all we ever do is abide in Jesus and soak up his good gifts but never share them, we're still not getting the full meaning of Jesus' call to abide. Over and over again in John 15:1-17, Jesus links abiding with "bearing fruit." As we know from Galatians 5:22-23, the fruit of the Spirit is "love, joy, peace, patience, kindness, goodness, faithfulness, gentleness, and self-control."

All of those fruits relate to the way we treat others. In James we read that if we see someone in need and say "go and be fed" but don't do anything for them, that's not enough. We need to help not only with words but with actions (James 2:15-16).

Sometimes that action is giving. I used to think giving of my money was the least I could do. Sometimes I've even decided not to give because it felt like a cop-out for not actually giving my time or other resources. However, after volunteering for a local organization the last few years, I've discovered money is so much more important than we think. These organizations cannot do what they do without money to support them. Yes, they need help and volunteers, but they also need funds to serve those they are called to help.

In the case of the local organization I work with, The Demand Project, helping the women and children who have been abused required a 24/7 commitment. Without monetary support, they can't rescue and restore those victims who have been abused. They can't commit their time to getting the survivors the counselors, support systems, facilities, and other resources the survivors need to begin healing. Yes, they need volunteers, but they also need money to do all the projects and outreach God has sent their way.

Today, pray about who you can help. Is there a local cause God has laid on your heart? Is there an international organization you feel a connection to? It is impossible to help everyone, but you can help someone.

As you look for an organization to support, do your research and make sure they are a 501(c)(3). This approval will ensure that the money you donate is being used appropriately and is tax deductible. You can also look up the organization on guidestar.org to learn how the organization spends their money and more about the organization's efforts to complete their mission.

I know it might feel like it's "too easy," but to do the work God has given them, many organizations need your support and resources. It doesn't matter if it is $5 or $500, every little bit adds up and helps one more person come to know God's love and be led to a relationship with him.

## *Abiding*

Today, spend some time praying about who you could help. Is it a group? An individual? Who comes to mind? Don't stop with prayer. If someone comes to mind, give while you're still thinking about it. If it's an organization, look up their website for your giving options. I like to set up auto giving. That way the organization can depend on my gift month in and month out.

# Chapter 32
# Helping Orphans and Widows

*"Pure and genuine religion in the sight of God the Father means caring for orphans and widows in their distress and refusing to let the world corrupt you."*

## JAMES 1:27

It is so easy during our sprint from sunrise to sunset to utterly miss those who have no one to care for them.

We like to forget verses like James 1:27 that give specific instructions about how we should act and who we should help. It's easier to say, "I'm not sure what God wants me to do or who he wants me to help."

This verse is explicit in how we are to help. Interestingly, it follows a long list of specific ways we can live out our life in Christ, and the admonition to not read God's word and walk away, but to do what it says.

If we know we should help orphans and widows in their distress, what does that look like? For some, it can be writing a card or stopping to visit some of the widows in your church. For others it might look like joining a Big Brother/Big Sister program to help struggling kids in your community.

I have friends who read these verses and became foster parents, even though it is a huge commitment and a difficult walk many, many days.

It can also look like showing hospitality to your kids' friends who are struggling at home, or inviting a widow over for coffee.

Caring for those in need can take many forms. As I'm learning more and more, God can do a lot with our little. Just this weekend a volunteer group I work with pulled weeds at a property that helps victims of abuse. Others in our group did some construction and painting. It felt like very little, but we all know how welcoming a landscaped and decorated home looks, especially to those who have never had it.

Today, as you think about how to abide in Jesus, consider those to whom you can reach out and share his love within your community.

## *Abiding*

Are there programs your church is already involved in that you could help with? Is there someone God has laid on your heart you can reach out to today? If so, write them down below and make a plan to act today on those ideas. If not, spend some time in prayer asking God to show you where you can help. Then jot down those names of widows and orphans in your church that come to mind.

# Chapter 33
# Reading through the Bible

*"Give ear, O my people, to my teaching;*
*incline your ears to the words of my mouth!*
*I will open my mouth in a parable;*
*I will utter dark sayings from of old,*
*things that we have heard and known,*
*that our fathers have told us."*

**PSALM 78:1-3**

Do you desire to read all of God's Word but don't know where to begin? Or have you started only to get lost in Numbers, Leviticus, or Deuteronomy?

We know reading the whole Bible through is important, and it helps us to get a good view of God's whole story.

During my quiet time, I've learned there are many ways to read through the Bible. Here are some of my favorites:

### Cover to Cover

You can read it cover to cover, which is a good way to understand the Bible as it is organized. The hard part about cover to cover can be getting lost in the books like Numbers or the Prophets who are harder to understand without context to their stories.

### Chronological Order

You can also use a chronological Bible. I like those because they make the reading flow together more like a story since the books and their chapters are arranged in the order they actually happened. Reading this way adds depth to those stories and can give you insights you didn't realize were there.

### Big Picture

There is also *The Story* by Max Lucado and Randy Frazee. It isn't the whole Bible, but it takes the biggest stories of the Bible, word-for-word, and puts them in chronological order to read more like a story. There are even discussion questions for each of the thirty-one chapters and scripture references at the end of the book. This book would be a great resource for those who wish to get a clearer picture of the whole Bible. There's even a parallel children's *The Story* for various ages.

Whichever way you try, it's amazing to read through God's story from beginning to end. There is a lot in the Bible that will both shock and surprise you. Parts of it read like the best action novel or like the steamiest romance, others like the gentlest love letter or the strongest war cry.

Even though most of it is more than two thousand years old, it's the most relevant book for our times.

Today grab your Bible and open to Genesis 1:1, "In the beginning…" and if you get caught up in the story, continue reading. Just 15 minutes a day, day-by-day. The rest of these abide ideas will be waiting here should you ever need them.

## *Abiding*

Which way will you try? Cover-to-cover, chronological Bible, or the Big Picture? No matter which way you try, as you read consider, what do you learn about God's character here? What surprised you that you hadn't noticed before?

**Resources:**

*The Story* by Max Lucado and Randy Frazee

*The Story for Teens*

*The Story for Kids* (ages 8+)

*The Story for Children* (ages 4+)

*The Story for Little Ones* (ages 2+)

Various Reading plans through Ligonier Ministries: https://www.ligonier.org/blog/bible-reading-plans/

*The One Year Chronological Bible* (various versions) published by Tyndale

*The Daily Bible* 365 readings with devotional thoughts by F. LaGard Smith

*The Chronological Study Bible* by Thomas Nelson

Even though most of it is more than two thousand years old, it's the most relevant book for our times.

# Chapter 34
## Praying "War Room" Prayers

*"I sought the Lord, and he answered me*
*and delivered me from all my fears."*

**PSALM 34:4**

Let's talk about "War Room" prayers. This type of prayer isn't new, but they do get their name from a recent movie, *War Room*, starring Priscilla Shirer.

In that movie, an older lady, Miss Clara, has a prayer closet she calls her "War Room." She goes there to pray for others and "do battle" on their behalf. She tapes her prayers and requests to the wall and then spends time in prayer over them. Through Miss Clara's examples, the movie shows how the prayers we pray in secret are powerful in our lives and the lives of others.

Not all of us have an entire closet we can go to, but there are many ways to create your own "space" where you go to pray for others. A paper or whiteboard on the wall, a prayer box full of notecards, a prayer journal, the notes section of your phone…can all be your personal War Room.

Prayer is powerful, and God promises he'll hear us (Psalm 34:4). If prayer is the key to unlocking the resources of heaven, as Priscilla Shirer calls it, I want to unlock all the resources I can in the lives of my friends and family.

Today, find a "space" for your own War Room. It can be a closet if you have one, a journal, a wall in your house, your car in the pickup line…you just need a space where you can go regularly to pray over others and ask God to be present in their lives.

Carrying others' prayers can be heavy work, and we can be tempted to take their anxiety and problems on ourselves. However, part of abiding in him is bringing others to Jesus. The more you abide, the more people will share their lives with you. As we hear others' stories, we don't have to be anxious for them, we just need to take their requests and problems to the one who wipes all anxiety away.

I'm praying for you today as you seek out your personal War Room.

*Abide*

Brainstorm below. Where could your War Room be? What times will you go there? Will you use a notebook for prayers? Random papers stuck on the wall? A dry erase board?

### Resources

*Peter's Perfect Prayer Place* by Stephen Kendrick and Alex Kendrick

*War Room* movie

*Pray the Word Journal* find it at: http://www.praythewordjournal.com/

# Chapter 35
# Finding Encouraging Websites

*"And though a man might prevail against*
*one who is alone, two will withstand him —*
*a threefold cord is not quickly broken."*

**ECCLESIASTES 4:12**

Did you know there are many good websites out there to help encourage you to abide in Jesus daily?

Some of my favorites are LoveGodGreatly.com, the First5 app, and If:Equip.com. The reason I like these studies is that they are written by women who understand where I'm at in life. The authors aren't preaching down to me but instead saying "Me, too!" All of these websites begin a new study every few months and go year round. They are also both FREE. You can purchase materials if you want to, but it's not a requirement to do the study.

What I love most about their studies is the built-in accountability. LoveGodGreatly uses Facebook groups to share and discuss, and First5 and If:Equip use an apps on your phone. I love these features since I know I have someone who will miss me if I don't "show up." I also enjoy reading what others have to say about the study each day. On days when I've been confused, their insight has brought understanding, and the ideas I have learned from the other women in the studies have often stuck with me for years afterward.

Today, check out these websites and apps. I've listed them and several others for you below. Try one or two until you find your favorite. Once you do, enjoy abiding in Jesus in a community of women whom you can share with and learn from. Love!

# *Abiding*

What websites and apps did you check out? Are you beginning one of the studies soon?

## Resources

Ifequip.com

LoveGodGreatly.com

Proverbs31.com: FirstFive app

Incourage.me

Shereadstruth.com and Hereadstruth.com

# Chapter 36
## Studying with Someone

*"Two are better than one, because
they have a good reward for their toil."*

**ECCLESIASTES 4:9**

When I was first beginning to have quiet time daily, it was so hard! I couldn't remember, couldn't find the time, or got distracted. Then some friends and I challenged each other to complete a study together. We would check up on each other to see how it was going, discuss what we were learning, and encourage each other when it got hard. At the end of the study, those who finished went out for lunch together. That study really helped me begin the habit of daily quiet time 20 years ago. My copy of that study we did together remains on my bookshelf to this day.

When you join with a friend and study God's Word together, you build a deeper relationship with God and with each other. It also helps introduce you to ideas you might never have thought about on your own.

Any of the previous study ideas would work for this type of study, but there are also Shereadstruth.com and Hereadstruth.com, *31 Prayers for My Husband* or *31 Prayers for My Wife* by Jennifer and Aaron Smith, and *You and Me Forever* by Francis and Lisa Chan that are specific to spouses.

If you're struggling to understand God's word and develop the habit of regular quiet time, grab someone close to you and study together.

Or if you already have a regular habit of daily quiet time, studying with a friend or spouse can help strengthen your relationship with them and God at the same time. You don't have to study at the same time of day but can study the same thing and talk about it later.

Today, connect with someone close to you and see if they would like to study with you. Consider some of the previous abiding suggestions and find one that works for both of you. Then watch how God blesses this time you both give to him.

## Abiding with Someone

Look through the previous Abide suggestions. Which one(s) might you try with a friend or significant other? Make a plan. When will you contact that person and invite them to begin studying with you regularly?

**Resources**

*Wise for Salvation* by Christie Thomas (kids 1-6 yrs.)

*40 Days with Jesus* by Christie Thomas (Kids all ages and parents)

*The Action Bible* (Kids 6+)

*The Jesus Storybook Bible* (Kids 2-8)

Hereadstruth.com and Shereadstruth.com

*31 Prayers for my Wife* and *31 Prayers for my Husband* by Jennifer and Aaron Smith

*You and Me Forever* by Francis and Lisa Chan

# Chapter 37
# Discovering the Context of the Bible

*"He established a testimony in Jacob*
*and appointed a law in Israel,*
*which he commanded our fathers*
*to teach to their children,"*

**PSALM 78:5**

To gain a deeper understanding of the Bible, it often helps to know the history of the writers and their original audience.

Recently, our church did a video series by Ray Vander Laan called *The Life and Ministry of the Messiah*. In one of the videos, Ray and his tour group sat at a gathering place in Colossae talking about Jesus' life as a builder. This video gave me new insight into many Bible passages. As he was there in Colossae, Ray talked about how Jesus probably traveled for his work and learned about many different people. He explained how Jesus' interactions with others shows in his parables and teaching. He listened to people and knew how to talk to them on their terms.

Realizing those truths gave new meaning to James 1:19 for me: "Everyone should be quick to listen, slow to speak, and slow to become angry...." Perhaps during all those years of his life Jesus worked as a builder, he was also listening to others' stories. Before he did big miracles or preached a sermon, he seems to have listened first.

Don't worry. You can study for years without knowing the history behind the books of the Bible you're reading. You can take it at face value and abide in Jesus and live a changed life.

However, learning the history behind the Bible gives a depth of knowledge and insight that can help make confusing passages clear. Or it can give familiar passages a new level of understanding.

Several Bibles have a history at the beginning of each book or throughout them like the Archaeological Bible. There are also websites like Biblica.com and biblicalarchaeology.org, biblestudytools.com, or the videos by Ran Vander Laan which our church watched.

If you would like a deeper insight into the Bible, begin with one of these resources and read the history of it today. You may be surprised by what you find.

## *Abiding*

Look up one of the websites listed in the resources section below. There is a lot to explore in each of these resources. If you're at a loss about where to start, I really like the En-Gedi Resource Center. Their resources on Jesus' Jewishness help to give new insight into ideas and stories that sometimes become rote.

After exploring some of the resources below, write down which resources you like the best. What did you learn from them?

## Resources

*En-Gedi Resource Center:* engediresourcecenter.com

*The Ecclesiastical History* by Eusebius of Caesarea

*The Story of Christianity* by Justo L. Gonzales

*Bible History Online* by Rusty Russell

# Chapter 38
# Sharing Hospitality

*"Contribute to the needs of the saints*
*and seek to show hospitality."*

**ROMANS 12:13**

Having friends into our home is one of my biggest struggles. Just today, I almost asked a friend to meet me at a splash pad because my house was such a disaster. Often, we think everything needs to look perfect or we have to have the perfect meal. In reality, I've felt most welcome into messy homes that looked just like mine! Sharing a cup of coffee on a couch while our kids run and play is usually when I've felt most relaxed in a friend's home.

Hospitality can be hard! However, part of loving them and abiding in Jesus is inviting others into our lives and into our space.

There are many instances in the Bible where the writers encourage us to be hospitable, to open our homes to those who need it.

In his first letter Peter writes:

"Show hospitality to one another without grumbling…whoever serves, as one who serves by the strength that God supplies—in order that in everything God may be glorified through Jesus Christ. To him belong glory and dominion forever and ever. Amen." (1 Peter 4:9, 11, NLT)

I find it comforting to know that when I move past my discomfort and am willing to open my home to others and serve in this way, the effort brings glory to God.

In her book, *The Life-Giving Table*, Sally Clarkson calls hospitality the "faith by feasting" concept. When we invite others into our lives and homes, when they feel welcomed and accepted, when their needs for food and relationship are met, then they will be more open to hearing about Jesus. They will be more open to what we have to say.

This idea is true even for our kids. When I am hospitable towards them and take the time for the small touches, the napkins, the candles, the hot chocolate on a cold morning, they are more likely to sit still for the Bible story than if I were to just gather them on the couch before bed.

Today, let's abide by welcoming others into our space and being hospitable, even if we're uncomfortable at first and our home is a wreck.

## *Abiding*

As you consider how to abide in Jesus today, begin with your family. How can you make tonight's meal more welcoming? It doesn't have to be fancy! One of my boys' favorite meals is a snack supper I got from Sally Clarkson's book, *The Life-Giving Table*: Summer sausage or lunch meat, cheeses, crackers, popcorn, and bread. They also love a little tea light candle in a jar that they can blow out after the meal.

Also, write down some names of friends you might invite into your home. Choose just one family or friend from your list and contact them today to make plans. Again, it doesn't have to be an elaborate meal. One of my favorite is Chicken Tortilla Soup in the Crock Pot that I share below. It's super fast and easy!

*Chicken Tortilla Soup*

4 chicken breast halves

(2) 15oz. cans of black beans (undrained)

(2) 15oz. cans of Mexican stewed tomatoes or Rotel

(1) cup salsa

(1) 4oz. can of chopped green chilies

(1) 14oz. can of tomato sauce

Tortilla Chips

2 cups grated cheese

Place the chicken breasts in the bottom of a crock pot. Pour the black beans, stewed tomatoes, salsa, green chilies, and tomato sauce over chicken. Cook in the crock pot 8 hrs on low (preferred method) or 4 hrs on high. Serve with Tortilla chips and cheese. Makes 6 servings.

## Resources

*The Life-Giving Home* by Sally Clarkson

Pinterest (great recipes—but don't get wrapped up in making things perfect)

We need to cling to him and ask him to wield the Sword on our behalf right when we feel the most like quitting and disconnecting from the vine, from abiding in Jesus.

# Chapter 39
## Using the Sword of Spirit

*"Finally, be strong in the Lord and in the strength of his might...*
*and take the helmet of salvation,*
*and the sword of the Spirit, which is the word of God,"*

**EPHESIANS 6:10, 17**

Many times I feel overwhelmed by life. Just last night I was feeling as if I was ill-equipped to even take care of my kids. They were arguing and disobeying, and my husband was working late. I had the grey cloud of depression hanging over me.

Satan loves days like that! They give him the opportunity to wreak havoc in the relationships that should be our places of safety. Those times when...

- we're overwhelmed by life, especially when it's more than just a hard day
- children are diagnosed with cancer
- we lose a family member unexpectedly
- financial trouble just won't stop
- sickness is crashing in one wave after another

Satan loves to take advantage of our weakened defenses.

But we have an offensive weapon against his attacks. God has not left us alone on this battle field. In Ephesians 6, Paul tells us that our battle is not against "flesh and blood, but against the rulers, against the authorities, against the cosmic powers over this present darkness" (Eph. 6:12, ESV). Then he lists all the defensive armor that we're given and ends with our offensive weapon, "the sword of the Spirit, which is the word of God" (Eph. 6:17).

Many of the ideas we've talked about in this book will help you get the Sword of the Spirit into your life. Bible memorization, listening to songs, studying the Bible, devotionals, podcasts... You need to connect with God's word regularly, so that when hard times come, you're equipped with the Sword of the Spirit.

Note, though, that it is the Sword of the Spirit not the Sword of Tara. It's not ours to fight with. It's His.

We need to cling to him and ask him to wield the Sword on our behalf right when we feel the most like quitting and disconnecting from the vine, from abiding in Jesus.

The very next verse in Ephesians 6 says, "praying at all times in the Spirit, with all prayer and supplication" (Eph. 6:18).

If you're having a rough day, or if you're in one of those seasons where it seems like the only light at the end of the tunnel is an oncoming train, turn to Jesus. Ask his Spirit to wield the sword on your behalf. Ask him to lead you and to bring across your path the verses, the song, the devotional you need to find encouragement in this moment. He loves to answer those types of prayers.

## *Abiding*

Today, begin by turning to Jesus for help. Ask him to wield the sword on your behalf. Ask him to connect you with the messages and words you need to fight the attack against you.

Often, I will look for verses to fight the enemy's attack, whatever it might be. Struggling with outside forces? Check out Psalm 18. Struggling with worry and the thoughts between your ears? Check out Philippians 4:6-8 or Matthew 6:25-34. Fighting crippling fear that won't let go? Read Psalm 33 and 34. From these passages and others you may find, write down and memorize a few verses to fight Satan's lies. And when the enemy comes and whispers in your ear, fight him with God's word and watch him flee. Write down the verses you found in the space below.

# Chapter 40
## Listening to God

*"But the Helper, the Holy Spirit, whom the Father will send
in my name, he will teach you all things and bring to your remembrance
all that I have said to you."*

### JOHN 14:26

Daily we have questions about what we should do in a situation, how we should parent our kids, and what choices to make. When we abide in Jesus we're already equipping ourselves to hear from his Spirit. In John, Jesus tells his disciples that his sheep, his followers, will follow him because they know his voice (10:3-5). Then in John 14, he tells us that the Spirit will remind us of the things Jesus taught (14:26).

God's Spirit gives us these reminders in many ways. Sometimes he'll bring an idea to mind while I'm studying his word or praying. At other times, a friend, Bible study leader, or author will say or write just the right thing, and I know it's a message from him right to me. At other times, ideas or thoughts come to me, and I know they could have come from nowhere else.

This happened a few months ago when I sent a text to ask my family to pray for my son and me. He was having a hard morning, and I was at a loss about what to do. During a heart-to-heart with him, I could feel the vibration of my phone as family members responded to my text with prayers. Then, instead of my usual disciplinary strategy, God's Spirit brought to mind to see my son and share the Gospel with him. This change made all the difference.

I told him I knew the way he was acting wasn't like him. We talked about how hard it is to be good and that's why Jesus came--to take away our sins and help us live better. We prayed together and asked Jesus to help him, and do you know what? The rest of our day went much smoother. I know that idea didn't come from me. I had read it in *Praying for Boys* by Brooke McGlothlin months before but had forgotten about it until God's Spirit brought it to mind at that moment.

What I want you to take away here is that to hear from God's Spirit and know his voice, you have to abide in Jesus. Sometimes ideas pop into my head, and they aren't from the Spirit. They're from my enemy who's trying to convince me to walk away from my family or a situation and give up. He whispers lies to me like, "It's too hard. You can't do this." However, since I spend time abiding in Jesus daily, I know who it is who is speaking to me. I know the message to give up in that moment isn't valid when I compare it to God's word.

That's why abiding is vital. We are made for connection and relationships—with each other and especially with Jesus. Just as you need to spend time with your friends to know them, you need to do the same with Jesus. He wants a relationship with you. One where you talk to him, and he speaks to you.

Today, begin by listening to his Spirit. Pray and ask for guidance in an area where you need it, then sit with him and his word and wait for the answer. It might not come in that moment, but trust an answer will come.

I'm praying for you today as you learn to listen to God's Spirit.

## *Abiding*

Today, ask God's Spirit for help in an area you're struggling with. Confess that you're not sure what you should do and that you need his help. He loves it when we acknowledge our need of him! Feel free to write out your prayer below, then wait for an answer.

If you feel a leaning one way or another, compare it with what you read in the Bible. Does it align with what you know to be true from God's word?

If you don't hear an answer in the moment, don't get discouraged. Often God brings resources, verses, friends... across my path in the following days, weeks, and months that speak right to the situation I brought before Him. As always, compare what you hear with God's word. He will never contradict himself. Use the space below to pray:

# Congratulations!

You did it! You have abided in Jesus in 40 different ways!

My prayer is that through these 40 ideas, you discovered ways to Abide in Jesus you hadn't considered before. I pray that your relationship with Jesus has grown deeper and that you now have a habit of abiding in him daily.

If you found the resources in this book helpful, you can find them all listed on the Resources page in the next section.

Even after you close this book, keep using these ways to abide in Jesus to help you live in his presence continually. Some days I use more of them, some days less, but keeping them in mind helps me stay connected no matter how busy or crazy life may be.

As we end, let's close out with a prayer:

*Jesus, thank you so much for coming to be our Savior -- The one who enables us to bear fruit and walk the journey to which you've called us. As we seek to abide in you, please meet us there. Please deepen our relationship with you and give us an understanding of what we hear and read. Help us to love others well, and give our hearts a desire for you, to know you more. Thank you so much for coming to our rescue and doing what we could not do for ourselves. In Jesus' name, Amen.*

# *Abiding with Kids*

## Chapter 1: Listening to the Bible

You can listen to the Bible together with your kids, too! While you're doing chores together, riding in the car, building with blocks, trying to go to sleep, let your kids choose some of their favorite Bible stories to listen to. The Gospels, Jonah, Esther, Ruth, Genesis… would all be good places to start!

## Chapter 2: Praying While Doing Chores

What chores will you do with your kids today? Who can you encourage them to pray for during that time? Begin with who they're serving by doing the chore. Cleaning the kitchen = their family; setting the table = the conversations that will take place; raking leaves = those who will play there… Write some of your ideas below for helping your kids pray through their chores.

## Chapter 3: Having Daily Devotionals

The important thing with kids is that you make daily devotionals fun and relaxing. From watching Jesus, I've learned it helps to meet physical needs first. Since I have three boys, I like to get them a drink and a snack, and then we sit down to read the devotional.

The YouVersion app also has plans you can do with older and younger kids, and I've added some of my current favorite kids' resources below. The important thing is to start. Find time today to begin teaching your kids to abide in Jesus, too.

## Children's Resources

*Our Daily Bread for Kids* by Crystal Bowman, Teri McKinley, and Luke Flowers (Kindle, too)
*Growing with God: 365 Daily Devos for Boys (Veggie Tales)*
*Wise for Salvation* by Christie Thomas
*3-Minute Devotionals for Girls: 180 Inspirational Readings for Young Hearts* by Janice Thompson
*For Girls Like You: A Devotional for Tweens* by Wynter Pitts

## Chapter 4: Listening to Christian Music

I love listening to music with my kids. If your kids are young, they might like artists like Go Fish Guys, Family Worship Seeds, or Slugs and Bugs. If they are older, introduce them to artists like Jeremy Camp, Hawk Nelson, and Toby Mac. Getting God in your kids' ears gives them a good soundtrack to play through their minds even when they aren't listening to the music. It also gives them good messages instead of the ones often found on popular radio. Your favorite music app or YouTube are good places to look for any of these artists. You'll find some of our family favorites in the resources below.

## Children's Resources

Seeds Family Worship
Go Fish Guys
Toby Mac

## Chapter 5: Practicing Patience

Kids find being patient just as hard, if not harder, than we do. Brainstorm with them a time when they are tempted to be impatient. Is it waiting for dinner, for their turn on a game, to go somewhere fun? What are some ways you can help them practice patience during that time? My boys struggle with waiting for dinner. To help, I have cheese and veggies available for snacks, or I might have them help with supper or set the table while they wait. Write down some of your ideas below.

## Chapter 6: Studying the Bible Using the LOOK Method

Depending on their ages, kids can use this method to help them study, too, or you can study together with this method. If your kids aren't writers or aren't writing well yet, you might want to just talk through the sections, or use the spaces below to record what you learn together.

*Listen:*

*Observe:*

*Open:*

*Keep:*

## Chapter 7: Praying ACTS Prayers

Kids can easily pray an ACTS prayer with you, but with a little rewording to make it easier to understand.

*God, I praise you because...*

*God, please forgive me for...*

*God, thank you for…*

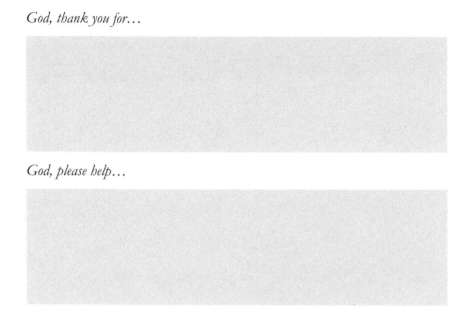

*God, please help…*

## Chapter 8: Discovering YouVersion Devotionals

I really love the YouVersion Kids app. When my kids wake up early, I often use it for their quiet time while I finish up my own quiet time. The kids' app has interactive Bible stories, games, and awards for reading and answering based on the stories. It is biblically sound and goes by the text, so it's a great way for kids to learn the details of the major Bible stories.

## Chapter 9: Joining a Church Family

Kids need the influence of a church that loves them too, even if they have two god-fearing parents at home and especially if they do not. If your kids have other adults or children at church they are close to, have them draw a picture for them or reach out in some way.

If they do not, consider what adults or children at church you would like to help your children connect with. Then invite them over, out to eat, or to the park to spend time getting to know your kids. If they are adults, you might even explain to them the purpose for their visit. It may take a few tries, but the effort will be worth it in the end.

Raising kids to love God takes a village, so work on building and strengthening your village today.

Who is already an influence in your kids' lives? How can you reach out to them to say thank you?

Who might you reach out to as you begin to build and/or broaden your village?

Kids: Who is special to YOU, and how can you serve them this week?

## Chapter 10: Serving Family

Children often see chores as a burden to endure. Jump in there and do the chore with them a couple of times. Whether they are three or thirteen, gently share the idea of how doing this service out of love draws us near to Jesus and teaches us to abide in his love. Like I mentioned in Chapter 2, when we do chores, it is a blessing to those we're serving. Teach them to pray for his help to do the chore with a good attitude and in his strength, not theirs.

## Chapter 11: Reading Psalm and Proverbs

Kids may need a bit more focus. Depending on your kids' interests and ages, you might begin with Psalms 1 or Proverbs 1:1-6. Once you make it through one book, you could do the other or switch back and forth. I've heard of one family even doing just 1-2 verses in Proverbs each day at breakfast and then discussing them. I loved this idea because it takes the pressure off for a long study in the morning, but it still gives our kids a strong start to their day, especially for older kids. Use the space below to note what you and your kids studied and learned today.

*Listen:*

*Observe:*

*Open:*

*Keep:*

## Chapter 12: Thanksgiving

My kids love games! In her book, *Prayer, In Practice*, J.L. Gerhardt talks about the "Blessing Game" where you act like you're in a video game and look back over yesterday to try and find as many blessings (aka points) as possible. My sons love Nintendo's character Mario, so we adapted it and call it the "Blessing Coin" game. We list all the blessings we can find to be thankful for today or yesterday. Each blessing is a coin, and we see who "wins" by finding the most blessings.

It's been fun to keep our lists and see how many blessings we have found to be thankful for. Try this idea with your own kids. See how many "coins" you find laying around that you didn't know were there.

Use the space to begin by writing down your blessings below!

## *Blessing Coin Game*

*Name*                                    *Name*

_____        _____

### Chapter 13: Finding Good Books

If your children are 14+, they might benefit from some of the books in the chapter's Resource section. Bible storybooks are also great choices for younger children. Find some of our family favorites below!

### Children's Resources:

*The Action Bible* by Doug Mass and Sergio Cariello (Kids 6+)

*The Jesus Storybook Bible* by Sally Lloyd-Jones and Jago (Kids 2-8)

*Candle Bible for Toddlers* by Juliet David and Helen Prole (Kids 0-4)

*Playtime Devotions* by Christine Harder Tangvald (Kids 0-2)

*100 Bible Heroes and 100 Bible Songs* by Stephen Elkins

*Pray and Play Bible* by Group Publishing (Kids 0-4)

*Unseen: The Armor of God for Kids* by Priscilla Shirer (Kids 6-10)

*Indescribable: 100 Devotions about God and Science* by Louie Giglio (Kids 5-10)

## Chapter 14: Journaling the Bible

Have your kids listen to or read their favorite Bible story and then draw pictures with you in the space below based on the story. They might draw what they learn about God, a picture of the characters, or how the story makes them feel. The story of Noah in Genesis 7-9, Esther in the book of Esther, or Daniel in the lion's den in Daniel 6 are some of our Old Testament favorites. Matthew, Mark, Luke, and John are also great places to begin for stories about Jesus. Or you might try an adult/kid coloring verse book like *Big and Little Coloring Devotional* by Rachel C. Swanson.

## Chapter 15: Learning to Listen

To teach your kids about listening, lead by example. Begin by listening well to them. Stories like the story of Abraham sacrificing Isaac in Gen. 22:1-19 or of young Jesus in the Temple in Luke 41-52 may be helpful for you and your kids. They show adults stopping to listen to children and the obedient response of the children, even if they may not agree or understand.

For older kids, you might introduce them to verses and stories like Abraham's in Genesis 18:16-33 or Hezekiah's in 2 Kings 20:1-11 where God even listened to people.

For all ages, consider having them choose a question to ask at the dinner table tonight, so they can get practice asking questions and listening to the answers. Some starter questions might be:

- What is your favorite book and why is it your favorite?
- What is your favorite childhood memory?
- Where would you most like to visit and why?
- Where did you first learn about God?
- What is your favorite song and why is it your favorite?

Sally Clarkson has a list of many more questions in the back of her book *The Lifegiving Table*. Our family took some of the questions like the ones above and the ones in the book and wrote them on popsicle sticks. We put the sticks in a jar on our kitchen table and pull one out every night (when we remember—wink!) to get the conversation going. Since we started, we've gotten to know one another much better.

## Chapter 16: Going Verse by Verse

Since kids don't have long attention spans, going through a passage verse-by-verse shows them how to abide well. If you are memorizing a verse together, start there. If not, open to Psalms or Proverbs to begin. There are great little nuggets in those books for children and adults alike.

Where did you begin? What did you learn today as a family?

## Chapter 17: Praying in the Car

I know it might seem awkward at first to pray together in the car, and if you have more than one kid, the who-goes-first fight may come up. (We take turns each morning.) But it will be well worth your effort. After a couple of years my, sons are comfortable praying, and I learn a lot about them and what's really on their hearts as they pray.

## Chapter 18: Listening to Lessons on Podcast or CD

Keys for Kids is a great podcast for kids. You can also find the Keys for Kids radio station streaming at KeysforKids.net. It has a lot of great music, studies, and stories to encourage your family.

## Chapter 19: Creating Art

Today my youngest son and I listened to bird calls. They reminded me that God gives each of us a unique song to sing. Then my son wanted me to record him singing, so we did. That video will now serve as a reminder of the lesson God taught us this morning.

What do your kids love to build and create with? Take some time today to go outside with them and learn about God from his creation together. Then recreate what you observe in some way.

I'd love to hear what you and your children learned about God today! Please share your thoughts and creations at #abidebook on Facebook and Instagram.

## Chapter 20: Being Kind

Oh goodness, this one can be hard! Some kids are naturally thoughtful, but most are not. Ask your kids for the names of two people they will see today. Have them plan ways they can be kind. Do they normally fight over a video game or toy? Have them plan to share. Do they go to school? Help them plan a way to be kind to their teacher or friends. Just like kindness takes practice for us, it takes practice and planning for our kids, too. Write their ideas in the space below and then check back in a few days and see how they did. What did they learn?

## Chapter 21: Memorizing Scripture

If your church has memory work for your kids, begin there. If not, you could begin with John 3:16. In the space below write down a few verses you might use to help your family begin memorizing verses together. I find it helpful to write these on our chalkboard in the kitchen, post them in the boys' rooms, and on their memory charts. I've even copied some of them and posted them around the boys' bathroom mirror. Anything to get God's word in front of them.

At my website (https://taralcole.com/memory-verse-charts-2/) I've included a copy of our memory verse chart. Feel free to copy it and use it for your family. I've used stickers or drawn stars when they've said their verse.

Also, one tip for kids: I started young. Even when they were just beginning to talk, I had them repeat the words after me. My youngest still does this, but by the end of the two weeks(-ish—it usually takes us a month), he can usually say the words himself.

I also don't require my older boys don't look at the verse as they say it. I figure repeating the verses 10 times really helps it to stick. They are still at the learning-to-read stage, so it helps with their reading mastery, too. We also talk about what the verse means. I want them to know the words, yes, but I also want them to have an idea of what it means or, if applicable, how to apply it today.

## Children's Resources

*SHARPEN Your Sword* 7-day Memory Verse E-course: taralcole.com/shop

GraceNotes, Kid Notes, and Man Notes (monthly memory verse subscription): gracenotessubscription.com

## Chapter 22: Doing Family Prayers

Did the ideas you tried in Chapter 22 work well for you? If so, great! Keep praying together regularly. You might record below how it's going during this season to look back on later for encouragement.

If not, choose another prayer idea from Chapter 22 or another chapter and try again. Just because something doesn't work well the first time, doesn't mean you should quit. Often I change how I abide in Jesus and how our family abides due to new seasons of life. That's why there are so many different suggestions in this book! Brainstorm some new ideas below and make a commitment for when you will try again.

## Chapter 23: Having Family Devotions

How are your devotional times going? Did the ideas you tried from Chapter 23 work well? If so, record below what is working and what you're learning from it.

If not, you might try another idea from Chapter 23 or other chapters in this book. Especially since we all have different learning styles, it can be a challenge to find ways to learn together as a family.

You might even need to rotate through several different types of devotionals or ways of abiding together. *Keys for Kids* podcast has worked well for several years with my family, but now the older kids want different material, so we're listening to videos from the *YouVersion* app, too. The important things is to be flexible and willing to adapt to new ages, seasons of life, and the needs of your family. You might also find my ebook I helped Christie Thomas with, *Sacred Pathways for Kids* helpful. It is like spiritual love languages for kids and helps teach you how to help them relate to God based on their personality type. *Below* brainstorm some other ideas you might try for family devotional time.

### Children's Resources

*Sacred Pathways for Kids* by Christie Thomas and Tara L. Cole—find it at taralcole.com/shop

### Chapter 24: Doing Service for Others

There are many ways you can get your family involved. When our family chooses Compassion International (www.compassion.com) children to sponsor, we let our sons pick the kids. When I take a meal to someone, I often let my sons help me prepare it and carry it to the door just like my Mom did with me. Kids like to help and they want to feel needed. When I serve in the nursery at church, my older sons like to help me. It ends up being a lot of fun! As your kids help you serve, they are meeting others' needs and laying a foundation for abiding in Jesus through service later on in life.

Kids may also have good ideas about service and may see needs that we miss. Ask them. Get them involved in serving others. Depending on their ages, make a meal for someone and take it to them. Draw a picture or write a card to encourage someone. Help mow a yard and weed flower beds. Help clean someone's house... there are so many possibilities. Make a plan, write it down, and date it in the space below. Then get going!

## Chapter 25: Discovering Bible Promises

It is so important to begin pointing our kids to the Bible's promises at an early age. It helps them see that the Bible isn't just a book of stories but applies to them right here, today. If they are having a particular struggle right now, have them help you look up Bible promises about that struggle. Maybe they are scared, feel alone, or are faced with a challenge.

Use a concordance, the search function in your Bible app like YouVersion or BibleStudyTool, or websites like biblestudytools.com or biblegateway.com to find the verses you need. Then write down a verse or two that sticks out the most. You can even have them color or paint the verse to make it their own and hang it in a place they can see it and be reminded of the promise.

## Chapter 26: Praying God's Word

Praying God's word can help your kids learn to focus on God and his word from an early age. If they are struggling, find a scripture for them to pray. When my son struggled with going to sleep after having a bad dream, I wrote out Psalms 33:20-22 and 34:4 for him. They are there by his bed to remind him and encourage him to turn to God for help.

Or maybe your kids need encouragement and need to be reminded of what's true about them from God's perspective. Ephesians, especially chapter 1, is full of those promises. Look through your Bible for some more promises today or look up the ones above. God promises that his word "will not return to Me empty, without accomplishing what I desire, and without succeeding in the matter for which I sent it" (Isaiah 55:11, NASB). Let's not forget that!

## Chapter 27: Delivering Daily Blessings

My kids love daily blessings! Recently I did a short email course with Christie Thomas called "Blessings" e-course. This course truly taught me the importance of saying a daily blessing over my kids and gave some good ideas of where to begin. My sons just light up when I put my hand on their heads and say their blessings over them at night. You can find her ecourse at: ChristieThomasWriter.com/shop.

You can also begin today with the blessing above or ones like: Joshua 1:9, Numbers 6:24-26, or Psalms 33:20-22 & 34:4. Basically, any verse can become a blessing if you add "May you…" to the beginning of it. Today, write down a blessing you can say over your kids tonight before bed. It can relate to a struggle they are having, a hope you have for them, or a promise they need to be reminded of. Write it in the space below.

## Children's Resources

*Blessings e-course* (christiethomaswriter.com/shop/)

## Chapter 28: Hunting Treasure

With kids you might make Treasure Hunting a little simpler, especially if they are young. Treasure Hunting can be anything from looking God's character, his promises, truths about him, truths about us… One of my friends and her kids looked for the names of Jesus in the Gospel of John as they read it. You'd be surprised just how many ways Jesus is referred to in John!

In other books, you may look for other ideas, such as: how do the people relate to God? How does God relate to them? What is their relationship with each other?

This idea may seem simple, but when going on a treasure hunt of this kind, you and your kids can learn a lot! Use the space below to record what you find.

## Chapter 29: Discovering the 5 W's and H

Still think about the 5Ws and H but have your kids use their favorite art, building, or craft to interact with the story. If they like building have them build the location and people. If they like acting, have them act out the story or a part of it. If they like play dough let them create a scene. Kids get so much more out of Bible stories when they can interact with them instead of just listening. If you want, you can share their creations on Instagram. I'd love to see them! Just tag me @taralcole and use the #abidebook hashtag.

### Children's Resources

*Sacred Pathways for Kids* by Christie Thomas with Tara Cole (taralcole.com/shop)

*9 Totally Awesome Ways to Read the Bible* by Christie Thomas (christiethomaswriter.com/shop)

## Chapter 30: Sharing Our God Stories

Make chronicling your God Stories a family affair! Depending on their ages and interests, you might draw pictures, journal, scrapbook, video, take pictures, but find some way to get down your family's God Stories.

As you begin, get down all the ones you can remember from the past. Was there a test your child was afraid they wouldn't pass, but God came through? Was there a difficult situation at school you saw God's hand in? Was someone sick and God provided in some way? Was there a situation where he provided just what you needed?

Keep your God Stories out in the open on a table or community device. That way it is easy to journal the new stories as they happen and refer to them when someone needs encouragement.

## Chapter 31: Giving to Others

Teaching kids to give their money to God from a young age is a good way to help them learn to be generous. I still remember my mom making us banks from baby food jars and teaching us to put some of our allowance in for giving, saving, and spending.

Getting your kids in the habit of giving regularly to church is a good place to start. If they have heard of an organization or individual from church that has sparked their interest, encourage them to help. Or if they have particular interests, there is almost always a related organization who gives to those in need.

Local food banks and missions are also a good place for kids to give. If they visit the place they are giving to, it helps them see the benefits right then instead of just dropping it in the collection plate on Sunday and seeing no immediate response.

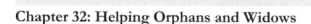

## Chapter 32: Helping Orphans and Widows

Consider how you can get your kids involved. Do they have friends that you could invite over for a special time together? Are there widows at your church they could make a card for? Is there a food bank in your community where you can take them to serve? Just because they are young doesn't mean they shouldn't help. Brainstorm with them for ideas of people and ways to help. Then write your ideas below and make a plan to start.

Sometimes kids are excited when they first hear the idea of helping others, but then they pull back when it's time to act. Others are unsure from the beginning. You could begin slowly. Have them write a note to someone instead of visit. They could pick out flowers and leave them on a doorstep instead of help plant them. You might even give your kids some incentive to help others as you begin. Possibly plan an ice cream stop on your way home. This would also be a good time to ask your child questions about what they did like: How did it make you feel? How do you think the other person felt? Really listen to their answers. Helping can be uncomfortable at first, but with practice, it gets easier over time.

## Chapter 33: Reading through the Bible

As you read with your kids you can ask the 5 Ws and H questions (who, what, where, when, why, and how). Their answers might surprise you!

*Young kids:* Who is in this story? What did they do?

*Elementary:* Who is in this story? What happened? Where did it happen? When did it happen? What can we learn about God?

*Older kids:* Who is in the story? What happened? Where did it happen? When did it happen? Why did they do/not do what was asked? How did their actions affect them and others? Who is God here? What do we learn about God? How might you respond if you were in that situation?

### Children's Resources:

*The Story for Teens* by Max Lucado and Randy Frazee

*The Story for Kids* (ages 8+)

*The Story for Children* (ages 4+)

*The Story for Little Ones* (ages 2+)

## Chapter 34: Praying "War Room" Prayers

Encouraging your kids to pray for others is a great way to begin to help them learn to think of others and serve them. Ask your kids where they would like to pray for others? Do they want to draw pictures? Write the prayers down? Take notes below and then make a plan to start.

## Children's Resources

*Peter's Perfect Prayer Place* by Stephen Kendrick and Alex Kendrick

## Chapter 35: Finding Encouraging Websites

For kids, I enjoy the Keys for Kids podcast. Christie Thomas has a lot of good ideas and resources on her YouTube channel: *Bedtime Devo Mama* and her website christiethomaswriter.com.

SheReadsTruth also has begun adding KidsReadTruth studies to some of their Bible studies. Check them out at KidsReadTruth.com.

If you do allow your kids to go online, please monitor their usage carefully. We use the parental controls on our Windows based computer and only allow them to view websites we pre-approve. Covent Eyes is also a good choice for older kids, and even adults. It monitors usage and sends reports to an accountability partner. Our kids' computer is also in a public area of the home to make it easier to monitor website use. On some mobile devices, you're able to limit website usage, too, and even remove the browser from the phone.

The internet has a lot of great resources, but we do need to be careful.

## Children's Resources

KidsReadTruth.com

## Chapter 36: Studying with Someone

Do you spend regular devotional time with your kids? If not, I've listed some of my favorite children's resources below. Pick one or two that look inviting and begin to spend time studying God's word.

Depending on their ages, your children could also begin to study with their peers or those younger than them. Maybe they could find a Bible or kid's study they like and ask some friends, even those who don't go to church, to join them. Perhaps they could volunteer to help in a children's Bible class or children's worship. There are so many ways for even our kids to study with others.

## Children's Resources

*Wise for Salvation* by Christie Thomas (kids 1-6 yrs.)

*40 Days with Jesus* by Christie Thomas (Kids all ages and parents)

*The Action Bible* (Kids 6+)

*The Jesus Storybook Bible* (Kids 2-8)

Kidsreadtruth.com

Keys for Kids Podcast by Keys for Kids Ministries

KeyforKids.com/shop

## Chapter 37: Discovering the Context of the Bible

Depending on the age of your kids, the resources for adults may work well. However, though interesting to us, that information is sometimes too deep for younger kids. Bibles like *The Children's Illustrated Bible* by Selina Hastings give good historical information along with the story. Another great resource I recently discovered is Kids Bible Maps at kidsbiblemaps.com. It has maps of many of the places and stories in the Bible, as well as Bible history. The information is short enough and formatted well for young children, while having expanded versions for your older kids. Win-win!

Did you check out the resources above? If so, what did you and your kids learn? How can you use these resources to deepen your regular study times? Did you find other great resources? I'd love to hear about them! Please share at ᵗᵗabidebook on social media.

### Children's Resources

*Kids Bible Maps:* kidsBiblemaps.com

*The Children's Illustrated Bible* by Selina Hastings

*Khan Academy* "Introduction to the Ancient Near East: https://www.khanacademy.org/humanities/ap-art-history/ancient-mediterranean-ap/ancient-near-east-a/a/introduction-to-the-ancient-near-east

*Museum of the Bible* "Jerusalem and Rome: Cultures in Context in the First Century CE": https://museumofthebible.org/exhibits/jerusalem-and-rome

*Museum of the Bible* "Collections":
https://museumofthebible.org/collections/artifacts

*Penn Museum* "Classroom Activities and Resources":
https://www.penn.museum/teachers-and-students/teacher-resources/other-resources

*Penn Museum* "The Digital Peen Museum":
https://www.penn.museum/collections/

*The Met* "The Met Collection":
https://www.metmuseum.org/art/collection

*Ancient Near East* "Kids/Youth":
http://www.ancientneareast.net/kids-youth/

## Chapter 38: Practicing Hospitality

Kids often love to provide special places for others. They need to be needed. As you're prepping the meal for your family or guests, ask them to set the table. Encourage them to look for a fun way to decorate the table. My kids love leaves, flowers, and branches from our back yard. It doesn't have to be fancy but something that brings joy to the creator. For me this looks like letting go of my perfection and Pinterest ideals and letting my boys be themselves in creative ways. When I release my idea of perfection, I'm much more open to receiving their ideas with joy.

As you're thinking of someone to invite over, ask your kids for their ideas, too. They are less inhibited by the filters we have and may think of a family or individual you may have overlooked.

## Chapter 39: Using the Sword of Spirit

Kids have hard days, too, and are in need of our grace. Often when we're having a hard day, they are right there with us but get overlooked as we're trying to survive ourselves. If they are struggling with a specific problem, look up verses about the situation. Google coloring pages for one of the verses and let them color it and hang it by their bed. Or if they like to build, have them build something that reminds them of the verse.

## Chapter 40: Listening to God

Share the above ideas with your kids. Often what we adults have a hard time grasping because of the way we've been raised, kids readily accept. Share with them that God's Spirit does help us and guide us. Share with them that when they feel they've heard from him they need to check it with what the Bible says.

For instance, is there a situation your child is struggling with right now? How can you both bring that situation to God and ask for His Spirit's guidance and help? Feel free to write or draw about the situation in the space below.

# Resources

## Chapter 1

1. YouVersion Bible app

## Chapter 3

1. *Hope for the Weary Mom Devotional* by Brooke McGlothlin and Stacey Thacker (Kindle version available)
2. *Power for Today* by Power for Today
3. YouVersion app
4. *God's Little Devotional Book for Women* by David C. Cook
5. *Our Daily Bread for Kids* by Crystal Bowman, Teri McKinley, and Luke Flowers (Kindle, too)
6. *Growing with God: 365 Daily Devos for Boys (Veggie Tales)*
7. *Wise for Salvation* by Christie Thomas
8. *3-Minute Devotionals for Girls: 180 Inspirational Readings for Young Hearts* by Janice Thompson
9. *For Girls Like You: A Devotional for Tweens* by Wynter Pitts

## Chapter 4

1. Point of Grace "Jesus Will Still Be There"
2. Toby Mac "Feel It"
3. "Nearer My God to Thee" by Sarah Fuller Adams
4. "Jesus Keep Me Near the Cross" by Fanny J. Crosby
5. KLOVE found at klove.com
6. AIR1 found at air1.com
7. KXOJ found at kxoj.com
8. Amazon Music
9. Spotify
10. iTunes
11. Point of Grace
12. Christy Nockels

13. Jeremy Camp
14. Hillsong Worship
15. Hawk Nelson
16. Toby Mac
17. Third Day
18. A Cappella
19. Vocal Union
20. Zoe Group
21. Seeds Family Worship
22. Go Fish Guys

## Chapter 8

1. YouVersion app
2. YouVersion Kids app

## Chapter 12

1. Hawk Nelson "Thank God for Something"
2. *Prayer in Practice* by J.L. Gerhardt

## Chapter 13

1. *Think Good* by J.L. Gerhardt
2. *Forgotten God* by Francis Chan
3. *Goodbye Regret* by Doris Swift
4. *Fresh Out of Amazing* by Stacey Thacker
5. *The Mom Walk* by Sally Clarkson
6. *The Action Bible* by Doug Mass and Sergio Cariello (Kids 6+)
7. *The Jesus Storybook Bible* by Sally Lloyd-Jones and Jago (Kids 2-8)
8. *Candle Bible for Toddlers* by Juliet David and Helen Prole (Kids 0-4)
9. *Playtime Devotions* by Christine Harder Tangvald (Kids 0-2)
10. *100 Bible Heroes and 100 Bible Songs* by Stephen Elkins
11. *Pray and Play Bible* by Group Publishing (Kids 0-4)
12. *Unseen: The Armor of God for Kids* by Priscilla Shirer (Kids 6-10)
13. *Indescribable: 100 Devotions about God and Science* by Louie Giglio (Kids 5-10)

## Chapter 14

1. DaySpring (they have many great Bible Journaling tools) dayspring.com
2. Michael's
3. *Inspire Bible*, NLT
4. {in}courage.com has many Bible Journaling tools, too.
5. *The Artisan Pace* by Jeana Saeedi (a coloring devotional)
6. *Big and Little Coloring Devotional* by Rachel Swanson

## Chapter 16

1. Priscilla Shirer

## Chapter 18

1. Keys for Kids found at: keysforkids.org/Programming/Keys-for-Kids-Daily-Devotional/Read-Listen
2. Keysforkids.org
3. *At Home with Sally* by Sally Clarkson, found at sallyclarkson.com/podcast
4. *Chatologie* by Angie Elkins found at chatologie.com
5. *The Glorious in the Mundane* by Christy Nockles found at christynockels.com/podcast
6. *Lifeway Devotions Vol. II* CD by Lifeway
7. *Abide in Christ* by Andrew Murray (reading of the book) found on itunes or other podcasting apps
8. *God Centered Mom* by Heather MacFadyen found at dontmomalone.com/podcast-show
9. *Out of the Ordinary* by Lisa-Jo Baker and Christy Purifoy found at outoftheordinarypodcast.com

## Chapter 21

1. *SHARPEN Your Sword* 7-day Memory Verse Ecourse: taralcole.come/shop
2. GraceNotes, Kid Notes, and Man Notes (monthly memory verse subscription): gracenotessubscription.com

## Chapter 22

1. *Peter's Perfect Prayer Place* by Stephen Kendrick and Alex Kendrick (3-7 yrs)
2. *Prayer Journal* by JL Gerhardt (7-12 yrs)
3. *Prayer in Practice* by JL Gerhard
4. *Made to Pray* by Christie Thomas (ebook available on her website: christiethomaswriter.com)
5. *Pray Like This: A Guided Prayer Journal for Kids* by Liz Millay

## Chapter 23

1. *Caught Up In A Story* by Sarah Clarkson
2. *Armor of God* by Priscilla Shirer
3. *Candle Bible for Toddlers* by Juliet David
4. *Playtime Devotions* by Christine Harder Tangvald
5. *100 Bible Heroes and 100 Bible Songs* by Stephen Elkins
6. *Pray and Play Bible* by Group Publishing
7. *The Jesus Storybook Bible* by Sally Lloyd-Jones and Jago
8. *The Armor of God for Young Kids* by Priscilla Shirer
9. *Wise for Salvation* by Christie Thomas
10. *Made to Pray* by Christie Thomas (ebook on her website: ChristieThomaswriter.com)
11. *Indescribable: 100 Devotions about God and Science* by Louie Giglio

## Chapter 25

1. *God's Inspirational Promise Book* with Max Lucado
2. *Joy for the Journey* by various authors
3. YouVersion App
4. Blue Letter Bible App
5. Bible Study Tool App
6. Biblestudytools.com
7. Biblegateway.com

## Chapter 26

1. *Praying for Boys* by Brooke McGlothlin.
2. *Be Strong in the Lord* and *The Lord is their Shepherd* both by Betsy Duffey and Laurie Myers.

3. *Pray the Word Journal* by Million Praying Moms at praythewordjournal.com

## Chapter 27

1. *Daily Blessings* by Susie Larson susielarson.com/email-subscription/
2. *Blessings Ecourse* by Christie Thomas (christiethomaswriter.com/shop)

## Chapter 28

1. YouVersion

## Chapter 29

1. *Sacred Pathways for Kids* by Christie Thomas with Tara Cole (taralcole.com/shop)

2. *9 Totally Awesome Ways to Read the Bible* by Christie Thomas (christiethomaswriter.com/shop)

## Chapter 30

1. God Stories on TaraLCole.com

## Chapter 31

1. The Demand Project

## Chapter 33

1. *The Story* by Max Lucado and Randy Frazee
2. *The Story for Teens*
3. *The Story for Kids* (ages 8+)
4. *The Story for Children* (ages 4+)
5. *The Story for Little Ones* (ages 2+)
6. Various Reading plans through Ligonier Ministries: https://www.ligonier.org/blog/bible-reading-plans/
7. *The One Year Chronological Bible* (various versions) published by Tyndale
8. *The Daily Bible* 365 readings with devotional thoughts by F. LaGard Smith
9. *The Chronological Study Bible* by Thomas Nelson

## Chapter 34

1. *Peter's Perfect Prayer Place* by Stephen Kendrick and Alex Kendrick
2. *War Room* movie Directed by Alex Kendrick
3. *Pray the Word Journal* found at praythewordjournal.com

## Chapter 35

1. First5 App
2. Ifequip.com
3. LoveGodGreatly.com
4. Proverbs31.com: FirstFive app
5. Incourage.me
6. Shereadstruth.com and Hereadstruth.com
7. Keysforkids.net
8. YouTube: Bedtime Devo Mama (Christie Thomas)
9. Kidsreadtruth.com

## Chapter 36

1. *Wise for Salvation* by Christie Thomas (kids 1-6 yrs.)
2. *40 Days with Jesus* by Christie Thomas (Kids all ages and parents)
3. *The Action Bible* (Kids 6+)
4. *The Jesus Storybook Bible* (Kids 2-8)
5. Hereadstruth.com and Shereadstruth.com
6. *31 Prayers for my Wife* and *31 Prayers for my Husband* by Jennifer and Aaron Smith
7. *You and Me Forever* by Francis and Lisa Chan
8. *Wise for Salvation* by Christie Thomas (kids 1-6 yrs.)
9. *40 Days with Jesus* by Christie Thomas (Kids all ages and parents)
10. *The Action Bible* Illustrated by Sergio Cariello(Kids 6+)
11. *The Jesus Storybook Bible* by Sally Lloyd-Jones and Jago (Kids 2-8)
12. Kidsreadtruth.com
13. Keys for Kids Podcast
14. KeyforKids.com/shop

## Chapter 37

1. *En-Gedi Resource Center:* engediresourcecenter.com
2. *The Ecclesiastical History* by Eusebius of Caesarea
3. *The Story of Christianity* by Justo L. Gonzales
4. *Bible History Online* by Rusty Russell
5. Kids Bible Maps: kidsBiblemaps.com
6. *The Children's Illustrated Bible* by Selina Hastings
7. *Khan Academy* "Introduction to the Ancient Near East: https://www.khanacademy.org/humanities/ap-art-history/ancient-mediterranean-ap/ancient-near-east-a/a/introduction-to-the-ancient-near-east
8. *Museum of the Bible* "Jerusalem and Rome: Cultures in Context in the First Century CE": https://museumofthebible.org/exhibits/jerusalem-and-rome
9. *Museum of the Bible* "Collections": https://museumofthebible.org/collections/artifacts
10. *Penn Museum* "Classroom Activities and Resources": https://www.penn.museum/teachers-and-students/teacher-resources/other-resources
11. *Penn Museum* "The Digital Peen Museum": https://www.penn.museum/collections/
12. *The Met* "The Met Collection": https://www.metmuseum.org/art/collection
13. *Ancient Near East* "Kids/Youth": http://www.ancientneareast.net/kids-youth/

## Chapter 38

1. *The Life-Giving Home* by Sally Clarkson

2. Pinterest

## Chapter 40

1. *Praying for Boys* by Brooke McGlothlin

# Notes

Introduction

1. "G3306 meno," Interlinear/Concordance, John 15:5, Blue Letter Bible app, accessed August 6, 2019.

Made in the USA
Monee, IL
14 December 2020